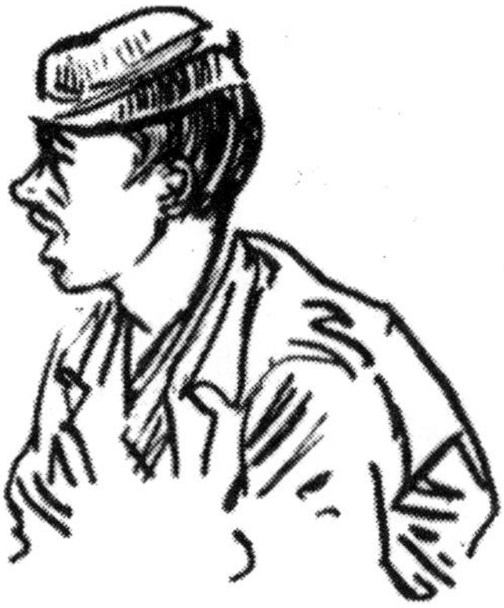

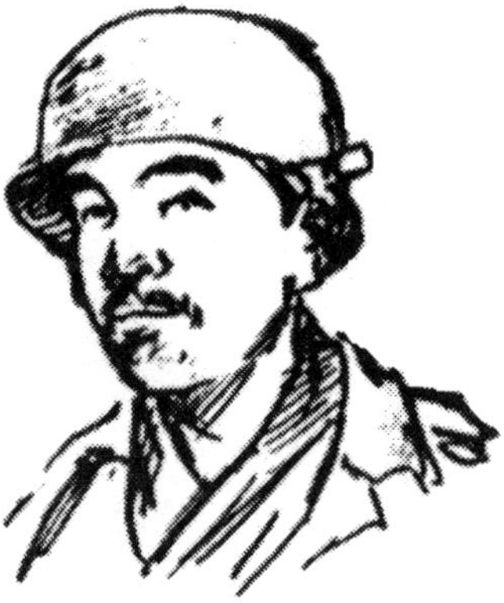

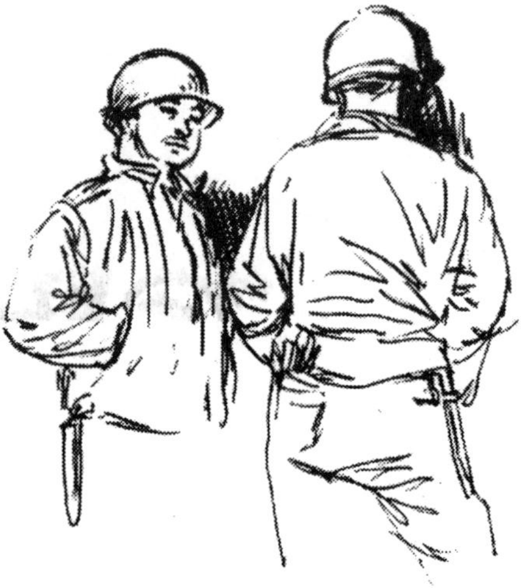

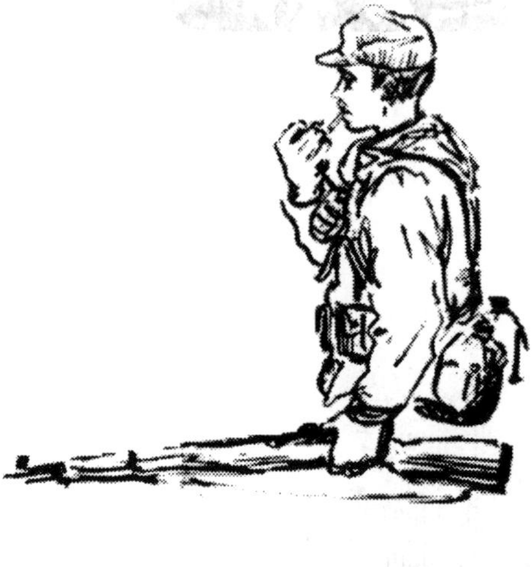

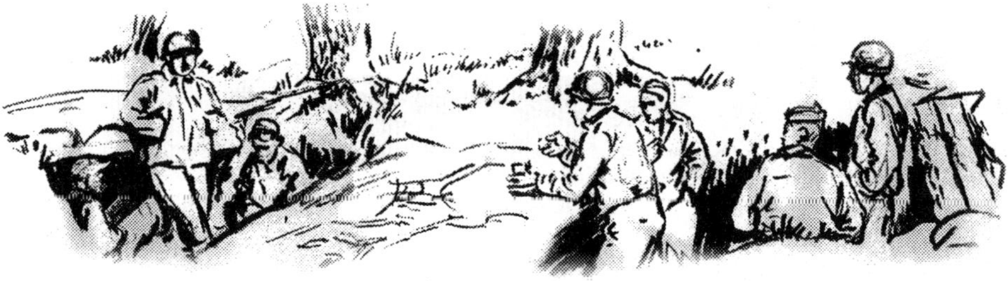

Mark Freedom **PAID**

Mark Freedom **PAID**

MARK
FREEDOM

PAID

Mark Freedom **PAID**

MARK FREEDOM PAID

A Combat Anthology

Lee Steedle
Editor

With over 60 Sketches and Maps by
Sam Kweskin
Illustrator

Publisher
83rd Chemical Mortar Battalion Veterans Association
Reno Toniolo
1826 Ridge Road
Jeannette, PA 15644

First Printing: July 1997
Second Printing: October 1998

Printed in the United States of America

ISBN: 0-9657649-0-7

Library of Congress Catalog Card Number: 97-60560

With special thanks to
Professor William J. Steedle
Art Department Chairman
State University of New York at Farmingdale,
for scanning, layout and electronic prepress production.

Dedication —

To those who died;

To those whose wounds remain;

their sacrifices

mark our freedom PAID

FOREWORD

Anyone unfamiliar with the Chemical Mortar used during World War II might guess it was designed for laying smoke screens. Although on rare occasions it did fire smoke shells, the 4.2-inch Chemical Mortar was a formidable big brother to the Infantry's 60mm and 81mm mortars. Unlike those smaller weapons whose barrels were smooth-bore tubes, the 4.2 had a rifled barrel like an artillery piece. Its heavy, spinning shell gave it great accuracy. The 4.2's 25-pound shell delivered more explosive power than the Artillery's standard weapon, the 105-howitzer, yet its launching mortar weighed only a little over 300 pounds. Because of the shells' high arcing trajectory, several rounds from each mortar were often in the air, on their way, just as the first arrived on target.

Moments after the shout "ROUNDS AWAY" was relayed from gun position to forward observer, the effect on attacking enemies caught on open ground could be catastrophic. 4.2 crews frequently succeeded in helping repel enemy troop concentrations during counter-attacks.

Along with day-to-day Infantry fire support missions, these accounts tell of the 83rd Chemical Mortar Battalion's five amphibious initial assaults plus an airborne landing, in close support of Darby's Rangers, British Commandos, and American Parachute Infantry.

— L.S.

INTRODUCTION

It is a pleasure to be asked to contribute some background to this Anthology of the personal combat experiences of about thirty members of the 83rd Chemical Mortar Battalion, with which I served as Commanding Officer from Anzio, Italy, to Innsbruck, Austria.

In the early 1940s world political problems dictated a rapid growth of all United States Armed Forces. Heavy mortars suitable for close tactical support were essentially non-existent, except for a few 4.2's within the skeleton of the 2nd Separate Chemical Battalion, located at Edgewood Arsenal, Maryland. This unit consisted only of one line Company, and an understaffed Headquarters and Headquarters Company.

This skeletal unit furnished cadre for four newly authorized heavy mortar Battalions: the 2nd, 3rd, 83rd and 84th. Other units were activated later.

The 83rd Chemical Mortar Battalion was born and trained at Fort Gordon, Georgia, as a close combat support unit. Its members reflected the best cross-section of male youth in America at that time. The 83rd amassed more than 500 combat days in the European Theatre of Operations. It was deactivated at the end of World War II. The exact dates and locations of the experiences chronicled in this collection can be located in official Department of Army records and within two 83rd documentations: Rounds Away and Muzzleblasts.

This Anthology presents perhaps a last opportunity to convey historical information to those coming after us. The emotionally-charged sketches of our highly talented battalion artist Sam Kweskin, the writing and editing skills of Lee Steedle, and the commitment of Reno Toniolo, current President of the 83rd Association, to publish this material, deserve appreciation and commendation.

Command, especially during combat operations, is a lonesome, awesome responsibility where there is no reward for failure. Let me state that the two former Commanders, Colonels Cunin and Hutchinson, conferred with this member just prior to their deaths, and both desired that the 83rd Association be informed of their personal feelings of honor and pride — certainly shared by myself — in having served with the 83rd.

— Colonel Sam Efnor, Jr.,(Ret.)

Illustrations

Index of Maps

Contents

*Mark Freedom **PAID***

Camp Gordon and Shipboard

Raymond (Pop) Hoover:

After previously serving four years in the Cavalry, I re-enlisted in the Army in 1941 at the age of 32. Most of the 83rd men were much younger, so I was quickly nicknamed "Pop".

One day on the firing range, a brand-new Second Lieutenant who knew nothing about the Browning Automatic Rifle told me I couldn't fire it left-handed, although this would have been natural, with me being left-handed. I had to prove to him that the BAR chamber, when emptied, kicked the shell out and not back, so that I and others like me could use the BAR easily and naturally. This became my weapon in later combat with "C" Company.

It helped me eventually to get promoted to Corporal, but I got de-striped for awhile after getting into a fistfight. It took a good while to get another stripe.

At Camp Gordon my wife Kathryn and I had one of those movie type scenes. She was coming to visit from Pennsylvania, having borrowed money for the train-fare from her boss. Kathryn was already on the train when word came down that the 83rd was shipping out, and all leaves were cancelled. I begged Lieutenant Rankin for a one-night pass, and got it. Kathryn and I had a big night on the town, and then spent the night together. At first light in the morning I had to tell her to get on the next train for home. It was three years before I saw Kathryn again.

Frederick W. Endlein:

They told us that the first Sergeant we had when we arrived at Camp Gordon had spent time in the German army before he came to the States. It was hard to understand what he was saying. When we would fall out in the morning for roll call, if we weren't fast enough for him, we understood him to say "If the door is closed — go through it!" That was a mistake. The next morning when we fell out, Kokomo came barreling out of the barracks and took the screen door with him. The screen went flying in one direction, and the wood frame in another. That was the last time the Sergeant gave that order. A carpenter had to install another door.

It was the time of year when it was quite cold outside. We were all pretty slow falling out for roll call. Some would wait until the last minute, and all they'd have on would be shoes, shorts and overcoat.

Sergeant Jack got wise to this and when we had fallen out one morning he made everyone take off his overcoat while we did calisthenics. We'd be standing there freezing in our shoes and shorts.

Reno Toniolo

A memorable night while crossing the Atlantic, enroute to North Africa. We were on the USS Monticello — formerly the Italian luxury liner Conte Grande, captured in South America — and the 83rd was designated for guard duty.

This particular night, I was assigned to guard the nurses' quarters. Absolutely no one other than guards was authorized to use that hallway other than the nurses themselves. While I was standing guard from midnight to 4:00 a.m. an on-duty sergeant came along and handed me an Atabrine pill, to ward off malaria. Atabrine tasted bitter, and I had no water to wash the pill down with. After trying unsuccessfully to swallow it a couple of times, I took the pill out of my mouth and threw it away. This, plus seasickness, had made me feel awful, and I sat down in the hallway.

Minutes later, along came a General, who proceeded to give me a good chewing-out. It wasn't my place to inquire how he happened to find me, so our inquiry was one-directional.

Although now, I have to wonder: What was our good General doing in the nurses' off-limits corridor at 3:00 a.m.? Not for an enlisted man — particularly while sitting down on guard duty — to question our peerless leader. Carry on, General!

North Africa

The 83rd Chemical Mortar Battalion — then known as the 83rd Chemical (Motorized) Battalion — left New York on April 29, 1943 on a ship renamed the U.S.S. Monticello, a captured Italian liner, and disembarked at Oran, Algeria, on May 11th.

Raymond (Pop) Hoover:

Sergeant Eisenburg got off a truck in downtown Oran with a couple of his men and said "It doesn't matter how many we see today, we're not saluting any officers!". As they walked down the street, the first officer they saw was a General — and they did not salute! They didn't get but a few yards when they heard the General bellow "ATTENTION!" When he queried the group and Sergeant Eisenburg as to why they didn't salute, the Sergeant explained what he had said to his men. The General congratulated Eisenburg for having such good command that the men listened to him. The General said "You're off the hook now, but from here on you will salute every Officer!"

Mike Codega:

Company "D" was in bivouac in a thicket of weeds near Algiers in preparation for Operation "Husky", the invasion of Sicily. I was ordered by Captain Ed Pike to post guards on our perimeter. I did.

"You and your Commanding Officer have not heard the end of this you [expletive].

3

Later that afternoon, upon hearing yelling coming from the direction of one of the posted guards, I proceeded to investigate. And there next to the dirt road that ran past our guard's position, was a command car with two officers standing up in it, one of whom was a General. The General pointed one of the pearl-handled revolvers he was famous for at the guard, and yelled "I'll kill the [expletive], I'll kill the [expletive]."

There was our guard, sitting with his back propped against a tree with his gun and an empty bottle alongside. His aide finally quieted the General, and as they drove off, the General yelled at me: "You and your Commanding Officer have not heard the end of this, you [expletive]!"

Before Captain Pike left our Company I asked him if he had heard anything more about the incident. He told me "No."

The guard's name is withheld here, as he was later lost in the Anzio LST incident. It is my own opinion that the General, as well as the guard, was drunk.

The Invasion of Sicily

The Operation Husky invasion of Sicily by the American Seventh Army commanded by Lieutenant General George Patton, Jr., and the British Eighth Army, commanded by Lieutenant General Bernard L. Montgomery, began during the early hours of July 10, 1943.

John P. McEvoy:

The first combat action for the 83rd was the landing at Gela, the site of Sicily's most carefully prepared defenses. Companies A, B, and C were assigned to the Ranger Force. Company D was assigned to support the 16th Infantry of the 1st Division.

Gela was on a ridge approximately 100 feet above a smooth white beach extending North and South for many miles. A level plain beyond Gela was approximately three miles deep. Beyond this plain the first slopes of broken rocky terrain extended into central Sicily, gradually rising until reaching Mt. Etna, a still active volcano

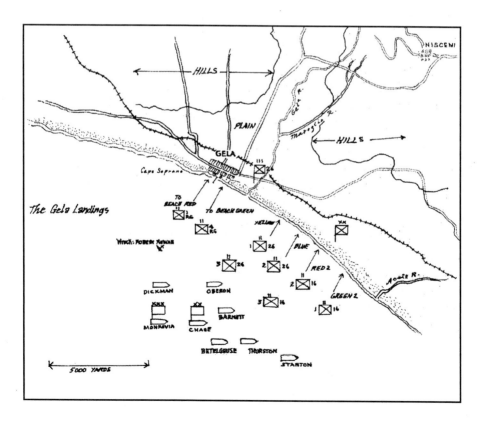

The Gela Landings

dominating central Sicily. A long 200-foot pier jutted out from the beach and provided some shelter for the local fishing fleet. A fort defending the beaches was at the northern edge of Gela and was occupied by Italian Coast Artillery.

The Rangers' task was to seize Gela and secure a beachhead to support reinforcements as they landed. Two companies of Rangers were to knock out the defending fort while the balance of the force occupied Gela and its high ground and defended it from counterattacks sure to follow.

Prior to loading in Algiers, several days before the assault, practice LCI (Landing Craft Infantry) landings were conducted. Six mortars for each platoon were loaded on the deck together with a limited number of munitions carts. Additional munitions were to be carried ashore by individuals — two rounds per person — in canvas carriers. Those two rounds added over 50 pounds to the normal individual gear that included a carbine, gas mask, shelter half, blanket, rations, and miscellaneous items.

The landing scheme was to drive the LCI onto the beach, lower the ramps, and the troops were to stream off, pulling the mortar and ammunition carts down the ramps, across the beaches, and to firing positions nearby. Trial runs established that the LCI could be unloaded in less than two minutes, Unfortunately the timing was done with the ramps extended horizontally onto flat harbor docks — a much simpler task than off-loading at night onto a hostile beach.

Some of our troops who were on transport ships had also practiced their off-loading. LCVPs (Landing Craft Vehicles/Personnel) were positioned by the sides of the transports, and the troops crawled down 20-30 feet of landing nets into the bouncing crafts below. After much tossing about in the sea, the LCVPs were lined up in waves, Each wave moved to the beach in a horizontal line parallel to the beach and landed simultaneously. When the ramp forming the front of the craft was dropped, everyone rushed onto and across the beach. If the landing was not dry you waded through the water to the beach. All exercises were conducted in full gear — a forty-pound load with weapons and ammunition.

William C. Ford:

Before we loaded on the L.C.I. Captain Burford came over to our Assembly Area and gave us a little pep talk — how we should do our duty and remember how and what we were trained to do. We were to go in with Colonel Darby's Rangers — the 1st, 3rd, and 4th Ranger

Battalions. Our battle gear included gas masks and gas protective clothing, because the Germans and Italians had not gone along with the Geneva Agreement not to use Chemical Warfare weapons. And of course, we had been particularly well trained in Chemical Warfare, considering the original design purpose of our 4.2 Chemical Mortars. We had a heavy load to carry ashore on our assault landing.

While training with the Rangers in Africa, we realized we'd be making an amphibious assault with them, but had no idea where. Only after we left port were we given definite instructions on where we were to land. It was to be on the beach at Gela, right in the middle of the city. The 3rd Infantry Division was to land to the left of the city, and the 1st Infantry Division was to land on the right. We were told that Sicily was well fortified with shore batteries all along the beach, but that the most fully developed defenses were at Gela because of its strategic importance, and that was why the Rangers had the difficult assignment of assaulting this key point. It was a very troubling time for each of us, since we had never been in combat before and didn't know what to expect.

As our convoy sailed toward Sicily, a raging storm came up, with high winds and rain. It tossed the LCI we were on in every direction. When the high waves would come, the LCI would go straight up, then come down suddenly and roll from side to side. The LCI was not designed to cut through the waves, but with its flat bottom it was supposed to ride on top of the water, which meant that it was tossed around in a storm. The nervous tension and the tossing ship took their toll in seasickness. We all vomited.

Finally there were hundreds of small landing crafts racing toward the beach on those high seas. Our LCI hit a sandbar quite some distance from the beach. The Navy, eager to get the troops unloaded, did not try to get us any closer to the beach.

When the ramp was let down for us to unload, every man grabbed his weapon tight. Sergeant Salvatore Sapio was the first man down the ramp, and I was the second. To our great surprise and confusion we found ourselves in water over our heads. We managed to struggle ashore. My weapon was wet, and I wondered if it would fire once I got ashore.

It was about 2:00 a.m. when we began to cross the long, sandy beach which was heavily mined, with obstacles of barbed wire. We reached a stone wall about six feet high. Suddenly three huge searchlights came on — as light as day. We all lay down at the base of the stone wall.

Our Navy ships, which had not fired up to this point, opened fire and shot out the lights.

Samuel Bundy, Jr.:

Our forward party landed in barges from the Pickman and were among the first to arrive on the beach at Gela. Lieutenant William Doughton was killed by a landmine. Lieutenant Laus and Sergeant Bonarck were first to leave our craft. Together they swam to shore. Bonarck was left on the beach to assist men from the water, and Lieutenant Laus returned to the LCI and advised men to leave excess equipment. He then reported the conditions on the beach. Many men gave assistance to those who could not swim, and somehow, no lives were lost in getting ashore. After the Company was organized, men returned to the beach under sniper fire, and retrieved mortars and equipment from the water. Soon after we left the craft, it was hit by artillery from shore. Private Kilpatrick received a face injury by an exploding mine. As quickly as possible, our mortar squads took positions, and communications were set up.

*We set up our mortars on the beach, close to the stone wall,
and began firing at close range.*

William C. Ford:

There were Rangers crawling over the wall where we were. Then the shore batteries opened up on our Navy ships just after the searchlights were shot out. I believe we had gotten across the beach before the enemy knew we were landing. The shore batteries were on the high cliff beyond the sea wall. It was now totally dark except for the shells from the shore batteries streaking bright red as they traveled through the air. Our destroyers and cruisers continued to fire. Red tracer bullets from enemy machine guns filled the air.

Machine guns opened up all around us and bullets spattered on deck.

We set up our mortars on the beach, close to the stone wall, and began firing at close range into the city. We fired on a building that we could see red tracer bullets coming from, and destroyed it. The Rangers continued to infiltrate into Gela, and destroyed most of the shore batteries along the beach.

The Germans began flying over our Navy and dive-bombing our ships. Some planes began dropping flares that lit up our ships for their dive-bombers. The enemy aircraft were flying everywhere, bombing and strafing.

Andrew C. Leech:

Our ship managed to pull close to shore and the bridge was dropped, but the water was still around our shoulders. We started to unload and the first mortar we dropped overboard went out of sight and was lost. A few men waded to shore, but we were forced back down in our compartments as machine guns opened up all around us and bullets spattered on deck.

A coastal battery opened up just across the pier from us and was firing point blank at us. He was shooting high and the big shells whistled just above our ship over our heads. Then, all of a sudden his range was adjusted and one shell came right through the side of the ship in our compartment. It continued on through, and blew the gun out of my hand and shook me up a bit, but no one was hurt. Then the second one came through a little higher and shrapnel flew everywhere. Kuykendall, who was standing close by me was hit — also Outlaw, O'Toole and Zookoski. They were carried below and we were forced out by the water filling up the compartment. When we got up on deck it was covered with people lying flat on their stomachs as the machine guns raked the deck.

Our naval guns were hammering away, shooting it out with them. The 20mm gun right above us ran out of ammunition and called for

"I tried to hold my rifle over my head,
when a great breaker took me, and I lost my rifle."

us to hand some up to them. We lined up and began passing up the ammo and singing "Praise the Lord and pass the ammunition" while the gunner fired away. He then was hit by shrapnel and was carried away and another boy replaced him.

Reno Toniolo:

On the invasion of Gela, the water was as rough as I have ever seen. To prove a point, years later I ran into a man who had been a skipper on a Victory ship, and had sailed the Pacific, the North Atlantic, and South Atlantic, and still he said that the waters during the Gela invasion were the roughest he had ever experienced. When we landed in the LCI-17, we hit a sandbar which I would guess was about seventy-five feet or so from the beach. That put the bow of the ship higher than normal. which made the landing ramp much steeper. We were to take the mortars on their hand-pulled carts down the ramp. Hawkins and I had the cart's tongue in front. Hawkins weighed about 130 pounds and I about 150 pounds, both trying to hold back the cart that was much more than twice our weight, and on a very wet ramp.

The two men behind the cart were to help hold it back. They told us they could not find the chains to hold it with, so Hawkins and I would run it from guard rail to guard rail, from side to side, trying to keep it from running over us. When we got almost to the water the tongue broke off.

Machine gun bullets were flying all over the place. I was carrying two hand grenades, one hundred and twenty rounds of ammunition, extra shoes and blankets, and we found the water to be over our heads! I tried to hold my rifle over my head, when a great big breaker took me, and I lost my rifle. How I got to the beach is beyond me. A pillbox was right in front of us, but they had caught the Italians sleeping. I used an Italian 25-calibre rifle for a few days.

Lawrence Powell:

When we came into shore, we hit a sandbar in deep water. I remember as I came up the ladder to the deck I saw a German searchlight shining on LCI-17. The brilliant light moved up the mast and showed the American flag waving. A sailor operating a machine gun on LCI-17 shot the light out. Captain Edwards had ordered all the men to get off the ship. Some went down the ramp. I jumped overboard with my full field pack, rifle and a helmet which was strapped to my chin. I could not swim, and I went down twice and came back up, hitting my helmet against the ship. Here is where Charles Carrullo had saved my life, and I will never forget him.

"I went down twice and came back up, hitting my helmet against the ship."

A lot of men soon had to swim back to the grounded boat to retrieve some of the guns and equipment we needed. Those I remember were Ed Krebs, Taylor, Kenny, Kozak, Tyma, Foran, Sereni, Spiranza, Plumly, Koring, and a lot more. After getting what we needed ashore, LCI-17 was hit by a German artillery shell. We got our gear together and we dragged our mortars out of Gela to an open field and dug our first real foxholes, and fired our first mortar shells.

Here is part of a poem about this event, written by Grace Rishell of the Pittsburgh Post Gazette:

> *Going into Sicily,*
> *his landing craft hit a sandbar.*
> *Forced to jump ship, Larry*
> *weighed down by a full field pack,*
> *helmet and rifle, went over the side*
> *and sank straight toward*
> *the bottom of the Mediterranean.*
> *He came up, no chance to breathe,*
> *then down again, up*
> *and down for the third time.*
> *When Larry woke up he was on the beach.*

He'd been next to, not an angel, but a lifeguard
from New Jersey named Corporal Carrullo, who had,
not wings, but a life saving certificate.

Moving inland, Larry helped set up
the mortars, four men for each gun.
The sound was so loud he broke
an eardrum but the shaking earth
was sweet beneath his feet.

During a lull in the fighting,
Corporal Carrullo tried to teach him
how to swim. Larry could never
get the hang of it... and the corporal
had to bring him in again.

Andrew C. Leech:

The Rangers and 39th Engineers were cleaning out the town, and when they went down a street they shot everything that got in the way.

A couple of Rangers with a bazooka got one tank.

Mark Freedom **PAID**

We began to bring in prisoners by this time, and everyone wanted to go out and bring some in. Even the cooks went out and rounded up a few.

When we got to another position we looked out on one of the highways and saw a cloud of dust that turned out to be a bunch of Jerry tanks approaching the town. We set up as quickly as we could and opened fire on them. We knocked out a couple and the rest retreated. Four of them had already slipped into town unnoticed and started to shoot up the town. A couple of Rangers shot a Jerry off a motorcycle and jumped on it with a bazooka and went out and got one tank. Then some of them got up in a three story building and shoved a charge of TNT out the window on a pole and got another tank. Colonel Darby of the Rangers and our own Colonel were said to have rushed down to the beach and secured a 37-mm anti-tank gun and got one more of them, and the last one was taken care of by Rangers running up behind and lobbing in hand grenades.

Samuel Bundy, Jr:

Small number of enemy tanks attacked, one was hit by our mortar fire, and burned. The remainder of the day was quiet except for German air attacks and occasional gunfire. Communication's men had much difficulty in operating. Combat wire was laid through Gela, and vehicles were incessantly cutting wire. As planes strafed, Cpl. Porea, Captain Edwards and his Headquarters Company personnel tumbled into a nearby dugout, which had once housed chickens.

This routine was constant, especially when tracers and flares lighted the sky. When planes flew over our positions we really hugged the ground.

Wofford L. Jackson:

I was just a few feet from First Sergeant Kedrousky when he got hit, his arm nearly blown off. The Hermann Goering Armored Division broke through on us, and all hell broke out. The tanks were raking us with machine-gun fire. I thought to hell with this.

Redheaded Sergeant Eli Johnson and I ran straight to the nearest ditch. I never saw Eli again. I think I ran several miles until I was completely exhausted.

Later I ran into Seymour Holstein and Doster. That night we got in a house with some 16th Infantry men. There was a huge barrel of vino in one room. Some of the men went out and surrendered. One of them was from the 83rd — Pfc. "X". After the war we learned that he had finally been liberated by the Russians, and that it took him a long time to get home. There was no way I was going to surrender until all that vino was gone.

That same night part of the 82nd Airborne Division came in over our Navy ships. The Navy shot down 26 of our own transports, killing 410 men. We thought this was just a German air raid until it started raining dead and wounded Paratroopers. Some of these made it okay. One was a boy from near my hometown, Manchester.

John P. McEvoy:

The view to the east beyond Gela was spectacular. A flat plain approximately three miles wide lay between Gela and the foothills that rose to the east. Although flat, some rolls running north and south could hide vehicles and troops. A simple network of roads led north and south and east toward the hills. All approaches could readily be observed. The troop convoys and naval escorts were scattered to the west. Landing craft operating from ship to shore could be seen clearly. By and large it was peaceful. Under the circumstances and excitement it felt slightly ominous. How soon, how many, and from where would they attack? But the size and distribution of our forces gave confidence during the wait.

A German ground attack was developing from the northwest. From our observation post we could see clearly that a substantial force was assembling. Folds in the ground concealed much of the movement, but blocks of troops could be observed. After a long period of time, groups of enemy soldiers began their advance across the fields. Time remained to get our mortars aimed and ready before they came into range: about 3,000 yards from our mortar positions.

When it was clear that they would soon come within range, preparations were made to fire a single round as close to their formations as estimation would permit. We wanted to hit them with heavy fire all at once rather than sniping at them one round at a time. All our training in how this was to be done was hastily reviewed and put into effect. All were alerted to the plan to fire one round and sense its relation to the target; then to take corrective action and fire two rounds from each of the four mortars in one platoon. At the time the first platoon fired, the second platoon would fire a sensing round, then make corrections and fire a supporting volley.

The enemy continued to advance on foot. The leading formation moved slowly and steadily while troops deeper in the rear moved forward to support positions. Time at last. The initial round was on its way. When it splashed close to the nearest troops they stopped initially then sporadically resumed their advance.

Then disaster struck them. Four more rounds landed in their midst, followed just seconds apart by a second, third, and fourth volley. Panic and retreat were immediate. The entire force reacted to the calamitous heavy fire. They got out of range and took cover spontaneously. Then a general retreat began. The rear troops pulled out too. The effect of our heavy mortar fire was instantaneous and deadly.

Complete surprise was attained, The enemy learned how devastating our heavy 4.2 mortars could be. Prisoners later said they felt that heavy navy guns had hit them. The Rangers learned on their part what outstanding defensive support they had acquired.

William C. Ford:

Once we had captured Gela and were on the outskirts of the city, we set up our mortars and began firing. But the enemy began to launch counterattack after counterattack, trying to force us off the beachhead. Their infantry was supported by tanks.

We destroyed several tanks with mortarfire.

German dive-bombers continued to bomb and strafe Navy ships that were trying to put men and equipment ashore. There were lots of ships burning. Just offshore, we could see huge black clouds of smoke, and we saw ships flaming.

The German planes began bombing and strafing our position. Our 4.2 mortar was the largest weapon our forces had ashore at that time. There were no anti-tank guns, no artillery, no tanks ashore. It was up to us to help destroy enemy tanks and blunt their infantry counter-attacks. The Rangers were patrolling and infiltrating enemy lines. We stripped our mortar squads to a few men each, so the others could help defend the city of Gela.

Soon the Rangers began to advance. Just ahead was a plain with farms growing oats and wheat. We moved forward and set up our mortars in a wheat field and fired in advance of the Rangers.

The Germans launched an all-out counter-attack against us, using tanks. We fired at the enemy, knocking out a number of tanks, and killing a lot of their infantry.

The German counter-attack overran the Ranger positions. We ran out of mortar ammunition, and had to pull back. We were cut off by the enemy, and had to make our way back down a drainage ditch to reach a defense perimeter around Gela. In spite of being strafed and dive-bombed, the Navy was able to put a few tanks and artillery pieces ashore during that night. There was bitter fighting all night long. One counter-attack after another. The enemy planes were bombing us continuously. We hadn't seen our own air force yet — not a single plane.

We had orders to hold Gela at all costs. There was a shortage of water and food.

Our order was to attack the next day, and we launched our attack at daybreak. The 26th Infantry Regiment had moved up during the night to our area, and launched the attack with our Rangers and ourselves. We met stiff resistance.

The enemy then launched their own attack against us using Mark III and Mark IV tanks, supported by infantry. The Hermann Goering Panzer Division, a full armored division was attacking us. Firing our mortars, we knocked out a number of tanks, and the 26th Infantry stopped some tanks with bazookas. It was a bitter fight, but we had to withdraw to our Gela defense line again.

The number of enemy planes over the beach area increased. We were warned by Army Corps Headquarters that the Germans might drop parachute troops behind us, and to stay alert for them.

Then the largest flight we had yet seen came over at about 8:00 p.m. Planes seemed to be approaching from every direction, flying very low. Anti-aircraft guns were firing from the Navy ships offshore. Confusion mounted as bomber after bomber roared overhead. Several planes caught fire in the air and sailed burning into the sea. One plane crashed near our gun position in the field. Then we discovered that these planes were our own C-47 transport planes loaded with the 504th Regiment of the 82nd Airborne Division. They were being shot down by our own Navy. The 82nd lost 23 planes loaded with men and equipment shot down by our own friendly fire. The plan had been for the paratroopers to land behind the airfield the German bombers were using.

Mike Codega:

The day after the enemy tank and infantry counter-attack in an attempt to push our forces back into the sea was repelled, Company "D" was ordered to take front line positions. We moved up.

We dropped our guns and slowly moved forward with hands above our heads.

It was late that night that Captain Ed Pike ordered me (Staff Sergeant) to recruit another man and go on patrol. "Patrol?" I asked. "Yes, you know. Go out in front of us, wander around a while and then return", replied the Captain (under my breath I added, "If we don't get captured or killed").

And so, "Sergeant Lombardi let's go — we're going on patrol".

"Patrol?", he asked. "Yeah, you know — like in the movies".

Since it was quite dark I suggested we not lose sight of each other, and added "We will go forward a hundred yards or so, circle, and then return." Which we did without incident.

As we reached our platoon's position, there was a yell: "Halt, who goes there?". My reply was "Codega and Lombardi". Back came a shout: "I've got a couple of dagos, I've got a couple of dagos. Drop your weapons and advance to be recognized!".

We dropped our guns and slowly moved forward with hands above our heads. All the while I'm yelling "We are Americans, you [expletive], don't get trigger happy".

It turned out that "D" Company had just been replaced by 1st

"The Army left nothing to chance..."

Division infantry. And so after satisfying the guard of our identity, we were allowed to rejoin our Company.

Robert E. Edwards:

Lieutenant Doughten hit a mine after landing at Gela. He was liaison officer for Company "A". His father, a V.P. at Whitman, sent boxes of Whitman's Chocolates to Company "A". A bitter-sweet memory.

Combat education — we were looking over the right part of the hill at Gela when a sniper bullet hit nearby. Everybody leaped for the foxhole. When the dust settled, I was the top man on the pile. So much for thinking I was quick on my feet!

I was then crawling under a truck when someone stepped on a land mine behind me. Shrapnel hit me in the buttock. Nice hole in seat of pants and impressive bloody bruise, but wasn't about to apply for Purple Heart and receive sympathy for a wound in the...WHERE?!

A famous officer with Stars on his helmet and collar, and those well-known pistols stopped me. "Are those your men without helmets?", he asked. "Yes, sir, our helmets were lost in the landing!", was responded, "Take a detail to the morgue, Captain, and get helmets for your men!" "Yes, sir!".

As the result of our having had to pull 24 men from the sea in Gela. I later lined up the men on the beach and had Company calisthenics. As the men exercised, they had to drop a piece of clothing when they miscued. Then the order was given to "Forward March!" and we had "sink or swim" survival lessons.

The Army left nothing to chance...they even assembled the Battalion to allow a medic to give directions for wiping the anus...lots of eyes rolled on that one.

William C. Ford:

Our casualty rate on the ground had been running high. We needed more men, water and food. But that night we got enough tanks and men ashore to surprise the enemy with an attack that was again led by the Rangers and 26th Infantry, with our mortar support. We did catch the enemy by surprise, and advanced across the long flat plain to the mountains. We moved along trails across high peaks and began the battle for Butera.

Andrew C. Leech

At two o'clock the next morning our artillery laid down a barrage on Butera for 30 minutes. There was only one approach up a winding road to this old fortress town located high on a mountaintop. The road that wound around the mountain had pillboxes and machine gun nests guarding it all the way.

The Rangers crept up these slopes just before daylight and with hand grenades and tommy guns blasted these men out of the pillboxes and dugouts all the way up the mountain. We started the long hike up the mountain behind them, pulling mortar carts, and boy, we almost gave out before we reached the top — which took us half a day.

Bill Gallagher:

I remember our skirmish at the town of Butera. Our first real close-range battle with the Germans and Italians together. Carlos Trautman and I were running a telephone line from the Command Post (CP) to the Observation Post (OP) when all hell broke loose. The enemy began firing at us with "skip" mortar rounds: shells that would bounce around like kangaroos. Luckily, Trautman and I jumped over a cliff overhang, and no sooner did we land than a big shell hit that same overhang and we found ourselves buried in earth up to our waists. I turned to Trautman and said "I guess we're finally in the war!", and he answered "For a moment I thought it was a beginning AND the end, in our first real battle!"

We finally reached the OP and our own mortars started to do a good job; the enemy came out of the wood-work carrying white flags.

Andrew C. Leech

As we took over the town the people seemed to be glad to see us. We broke open a church door where the Germans had a lot of food stored up which they had taken from the Italians. We told the people to come and get it. There was a mad rush for it until it had all been carried away. They gave us water, almonds and wine.

We stayed that night in an old Italian bivouac area and the fleas like to have eaten us up. We stayed here about three days and then started the drive up the coast, taking town after town and lots of prisoners. As the Germans retreated ahead of us they would pull out and leave the Italians to hold. The Italians would fire a few rounds and give up. Sometimes they would change into civilian clothes which was okay with us if they didn't cause any trouble.

Mike Codega:

Pfc. Bellomo said he had relatives in Sciacca who were fishermen. We were bivouacked a few miles south of Sciacca and Pfc. Bellomo requested permission to go to that village to try to locate his relatives. On his return he said he did find them and that they had invited our Company for a sardine cook-out on the beach.

And so on the appointed day, our Captain Ed Pike thought the Company should go for a hike to the beach of Sciacca.

We arrived without incident, and there to greet us were several fishermen, all relatives of Bellomo. And also there on the sand were several jugs of red wine, loaves of hard, dark bread, and sardines being broiled on large boulders next to a roaring fire. A good time was had by all!

Sam Bundy:

Headquarters took over a creamery in Mazera del Vallo. Here we had a fair set up — nice building, white walls, tile floors. Hired a private washerwoman. Sick bay for malaria patients was established in town, where we were in complete charge under a Major Hildebrand. It was temporary M.P. detail. City Hall building was our headquarters. In a couple of days we moved into a modern school building located in center of town, with a couple dozen large rooms at our disposal. We lived comfortably. Showers were set up. Italian boys kept building clean for a few cigarettes a day.

One plane dropped a bomb very close beside our small ship.

We secured grain from other towns to feed the people here in Mazera del Vallo. Several raids were made to find hoarded food, merchandise, and military equipment. Ammo dumps were reported to us, which we disposed of. Black market was checked. Swimming, fishing, and eating ice cream and cake were favorite pastimes of most of the men. Vito, our best Italian worker, stood reveille and exercised with us in the morning, and worked in our kitchen the remainder of the day. A price list was posted in town to eliminate overcharging. Shave and haircut was only six cents. Received our first Allied Military Currency here. Jewelry shops did a bang-up business, and could Captain Edwards keep the prices down!

On September 9th we moved through Palermo to Termini. Here we received our replacements: four new officers, and fifty men from the First Division. Lieutenant O'Connor was the only officer who remained with us. Colonel Cunin transferred out of our Battalion. Captain Edwards transferred to Headquarters Staff, for Lieutenant McEvoy, our new C.O. Here we trained and fired mortars several times. Silver Stars to Corporal Bishop and Sergeant Bonarek.

William C. Ford:

After we captured Palermo, the enemy had set up a strong defense along the coastal road to Mt. Etna and Messina. A frontal approach across the long, flat plains that lay before Messina, would have been an invitation to slaughter whoever entered them.

"C" and "B" Companies were pulled off the line, and attached to the 179th Infantry Regiment of the 45th Division, to make an amphibious assault around Cape Orlando, circling behind enemy lines. We loaded on an LCI. Although it was a short sail, enemy aircraft spotted our convoy. Their planes dropped a lot of bombs.

The LCI we were on wasn't hit, but one plane dropped a bomb very close beside our small ship.

When we began unloading off the LCI onto the beach we came upon many land mines, but encountered only light, rear-guard small arms fire. It became apparent that the enemy, aware of our end-run around their coastal position, had pulled back inland, to avoid being cut off or surrounded. We made contact with the 3rd Infantry Division. We advanced with the 3rd toward Messina. We met very little resistance, and found only a few snipers trying to delay us as much as possible. On August 17th, with the 3rd Division, we were the first Allied troops to enter Messina. The enemy had departed for the Italian mainland by way of the Straits of Messina, just about four hours before we entered the city. Sicily now belonged to the Allies!

Pozzuoli
Naples
Vesuvius
Avellino
Battipaglia
Maori
Chiunzi Pass
Sorrento Pen.
Salerno
Rangers/83rd
British Commando
British 46 Div.
British 56 Div.
American 36th Div.
Calore River
Paestum

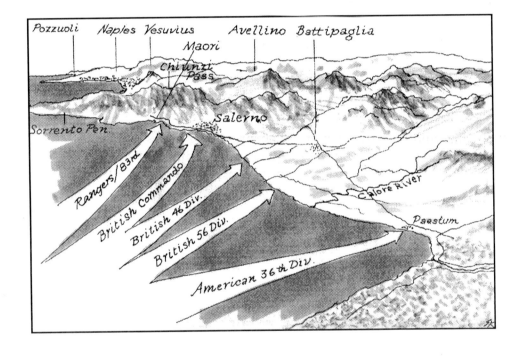

THE INVASION OF ITALY

Although the Italian government had secretly surrendered unconditionally to the Allies September 3rd, 1943, the much better trained and organized Germans saw the rugged, mountainous boot of Italy as ideal defensive terrain, and were determined to hold the Italian mainland at all costs.

The British 8th Army had crossed the Straits of Messina to the toe of Italy, while the main Allied assault was launched over a twenty-five mile wide area in the Gulf of Salerno to the north. To protect the left flank of the Fifth Army landing on beaches south of Salerno on September 9th, a task force comprised of the lst, 3rd, and 4th Ranger Battalions, supported by Company "C" of the 83rd, landed at Maiori; while the British 2nd and 41st Commandos, supported by the 83rd's Company "D" landed at Vietri-sul-Mare.

William C. Ford:

Darby's Rangers and "C" Company of the 83rd landed at Maiori at 2:00 a.m., and held the element of surprise. There was no naval bombardment nor air attack to support our landing. But Navy gunfire supported us by suppressing enemy installations after all assault elements were ashore.

The enemy reached our gun position a number of times, throwing hand grenades and firing burp-guns.

We advanced rapidly, meeting only light opposition from enemy outposts. We fought our way up the high, rugged mountain that had only narrow roads and trails. At daylight we crossed small lemon and orange orchards and vineyards. Our objective was to capture and occupy the high ridge and peaks at Chiunzi Pass inland.

Before we reached our objective we received heavy machine gun and burp-gun fire from the enemy. By afternoon we reached the peak on what was a critical supply road for the Germans. Our first platoon set up our mortars on the right side of the road; the second platoon to the left. Due to the high mountain peaks, our army artillery and naval guns could not reach the enemy, who were safely in defilade. We began firing on the enemy movements of troops, tanks and supplies moving up along this highway.

We kept the highway under continuous shelling, destroying a lot of their equipment. The Rangers had a half-track with a 105 artillery gun mounted on it. They would pull the half-track up in the pass and fire four or five rounds, then back it to a safe position down the mountain road.

Due to its tactical importance, we had to hold on to the position we had captured, and our mortars continued to shell the highway day and night. Our entire sector began receiving continuous counter-attacks, and mortar and artillery fire. It had been planned that we were to hold this position for three days, but because the 5th and 8th Armies did not advance as scheduled, we were ultimately to hold our position for eighteen days. The following day, the German planes came over and bombed and strafed our position. One plane dropped propaganda leaflets describing Salerno as a death trap. The enemy soon had our position under continuous mortar and artillery fire. The enemy had a mortar battery set up in a high, rocky area just at the foot of the mountain. We continuously tried to knock this position out. We would silence them for a short while, but soon came under shell-fire again.

We couldn't avoid leaving wide open spaces in our lines because of the amount of territory we were trying to hold.

The Germans were able to infiltrate our lines. The enemy reached our gun position a number of times, throwing hand grenades and firing burp-guns. The situation became critical, and every individual felt this.

We moved our mortars some 500 yards to the right of the pass. In this high, rocky area, it was harder for the enemy to shell our position. But we had a problem of getting ammunition to this gun position. We stripped all gun crews to just three men. The others would take up positions as riflemen, or carry ammunition from the road to our new gun position. We had a back pack that enabled us to carry two 25-pound shells at a time. We would rotate from rifle position to gun position to ammunition carrier. Our holding this position at Chiunzi Pass was so vital for flank security of the Fifth Army that we had orders to hold it at all cost. The Rangers were continuously on patrol duty, but we shared this duty. We fought side-by-side with the Rangers, filling in the huge holes in our lines. Our water and food supply was short. We would take only one swallow of water at a time. We didn't know when we might get more water.

Our food was C-rations, consisting daily of dried eggs for breakfast, one can of beans for dinner, and one can of potato hash for supper. Our emergency K-rations were very small — we could carry them in our pocket, and they consisted of one can of cheese and one of dried eggs.

Our casualties began to run high. William Hamilton, a very close friend of mine from Oxford, Mississippi was killed.

One day when the enemy was shelling our position, the explosions had a very peculiar odor. Sergeant Sapio thought we were under a chemical gas attack. He yelled "GAS!" and we all put on our gas masks. At this time of the war, the Germans had not agreed to the Geneva agreement not to use chemical warfare. We all carried gas masks and chemically-treated clothing. But soon we were given the "All Clear" —- no gas attack. Across the valley from our position we could see Mt. Vesuvius, and that there was a blast of red fire coming from that volcano. We could see the lava flowing down the mountain. Some days the wind blew ashes and odors to us from the volcano.

The enemy was making every effort to destroy us, because we had interrupted their supply line to the valley. Also, if the enemy could drive us off Chiunzi Pass, they could drive behind our Fifth Army lines. It was very important for us to hold on to the Pass. Once, after they had counter-attacked strongly the night before, we found in the daylight that the enemy had infiltrated our lines and had us surrounded. We were fighting SS-infantry that was firing burp-guns and throwing hand grenades into our position. We soon killed or captured all of them. But only a short time later they counter-attacked us again, and we had another bitter fight. The entire eighteen days at Chiunzi Pass we faced one counter-attack after another, but we continued to keep the German supply route under

A Commando walked up to it and dropped a grenade in.

our mortar fire. Finally the American Fifth Army and the British
Eighth Army began to advance up the valley toward us at the Pass.

On September 27th we received reinforcements to attack, after we
prepared a heavy mortar barrage on the enemy positions and their
supply route. The Darby Rangers attacked and overran the enemy
positions, and advanced through Castellamare to enter the plains of
Naples.

With British Sherman tank support we advanced a little at a time
along small trails and through orchards. The German snipers were
hidden behind stone walls, so we were dropping mortar shells just
over these walls ahead of the rifle company. The riflemen then tossed
grenades over the walls as they advanced. Soon all the surrounding
area was cleared and occupied. The road was now open for tanks to
advance.

Wofford L. Jackson:

We landed north of the main invasion force 30 minutes before
H-Hour with the 41st Royal Marine Commandos. Their Commanding
Officer was "Mad Jack" Churchill, the son of Winston. As we arrived
off the coast we were attacked by air but our anti-aircraft gunners
did a good job of driving the planes off. Down below deck it sounded
like all hell was breaking loose. I had to go to the toilet every few
minutes. After a while I decided, what the hell am I keeping these
pants dry for? They will get wet when they sink us anyway. Pat
Renfroe had a World War I trench knife. It was a dagger on brass
knuckles. I tried to buy it from him, but he wouldn't sell. During the
worst noise overhead he came over to my bunk and said: "Jackson,
you always wanted this knife — here, you can have it!"

We made the landing in a small village — Vietri-sul-Mare. It was no
small feat, getting heavy mortar carts down the ramp of our LCI. We
immediately made for high ground and ran smack into a German
tank with the motor running. The crew inside must have been drunk
or asleep. We were single file pulling mortar carts, and they could
have wiped us all out with just a few shots. A Commando walked up
to it and dropped a grenade in. No Germans came out. The tank blew
up for 30 minutes. By daylight I had already liberated several bottles
of Marsala and made friends with several Italian civilians.

We emplaced in the middle of town where we had to fire in all
directions except toward the sea. We were also receiving fire of all
kinds from all of those directions.

Vietri is at the south end of the Amalfi Drive. We had casualties
every day. Some mortar crews actually operated with only two men.
Three-man crews were about what most squads had left.

One day Sergeant James Lauro (who later got a battlefield
commission to Second Lieutenant) was directing fire onto two tanks
that were attacking us from the south. One German shell made a
direct hit on a Commando there with him. It blew blood, guts and
everything else all over Lauro. The only thing it did to him, it blew
the end of his trigger finger off. Lauro was an atheist. I asked him if
he prayed. He said "There is no God". I said "Yes there is, and He's
trying to tell you something!"

Some of the Commandos had goatees. A few of our men started
growing them too. One of the best was on Pfc. Gulley. His name is not
on our fatality list, but should be. His head was blown off down to his
lower lip and goatee. When the sun came up the next morning, there

wasn't a goatee in sight. Sergeant Codega had grown a nice one, and it was gone too.

One boy who was dead didn't have a wound mark on him. One man still standing with his guts hanging out was saying over and over "I'm too young to die." When he fell, he did.

One night the First Platoon led by Lieutenant Miller and Lieutenant Beasly came by our position. They said an Italian had told them there were some Germans up the road who wanted to surrender. But we knew there was a machine gun up there that we never could knock out. The officers were smart enough to hold their platoon back while they themselves tackled the Germans. They contacted them all right. Our officers' bodies lay by the road up there for days. Finally the Germans buried Lieutenant Beasly but left Lieutenant Miller there to rot because he was a Jew!

At Vietri we had about run out of officers who could direct fire. Sergeant Codega had to do most of it, and was good at it. At one time he and the German fire director were staring at each other through their binoculars, face to face.

We ran out of 4.2 ammo and had to take up our rifles with the Commandos. One Commando offered me a bayonet. I told him never mind, if it came to that, I wouldn't need it. All I would have to do was reach in my pants, get a handful, and blind hell out of the German!

We heard a rumor they were sending everything that would float, from Sicily and North Africa to evacuate our beachhead. But we had already been told that the ships that brought us there would not take us off. Colonel Churchill had told our officers we would fight there to the last man. I thought that would sound good in the movies, and for a while it was just like the movies.

During one bad time, we just about had to abandon our wounded, and fight like hell with our rifles. My best drinking buddy, Charlie Vance had been killed. I took his rifle and ammo and laid it on a mortar cart. Along came a Commando medic who wanted a weapon. I reminded him if a medic is caught with a weapon he would be killed. He said "Give me the rifle — we're all going to be killed anyway". The last I saw him, he was up on a rooftop firing like hell. When we left Vietri you couldn't find a square foot of ground where there wasn't a piece of shrapnel.

We had one more mission in that area. After British Infantry took over Vietri, British trucks were sent for us to help stop a German counterattack on the main beach forces. We had been resupplied with mortar ammo and we were set up in front of massive artillery batteries and some Infantry. The Germans were massing for an all-out attack. We had time to prepare hundreds of rounds of ammo, all with the same number of powder rings. The distances to our targets were adjusted by either lowering or raising barrel elevations. When the signal to fire came, everything on the beachhead, even ships offshore, opened up. Hundreds of Germans were killed or wounded. I'm sure our mortars got our share. That massive barrage broke the back of the enemy. The beachhead was finally secure.

Mike Codega:

Dry British humor: a couple of days after landing at Vietre-sul-Mare in support of the 41st and 2nd British Commandos, our commanding officer Captain Ed Pike received word to report to the 2nd Commando headquarters.

As Captain Pike and I entered the building, the enemy began shelling the area. Came a shout from a big red mustachioed officer: "Yanks, go back out and come back in walking backwards — the enemy will think you're leaving and will stop their shelling!" That officer, Major Randolph Churchill, was the son of England's Prime Minister.

William C. Ford:

We had another hard battle, moving toward Naples. The thick rock walls enabled the Germans to emplace machine guns, mortars, and snipers, and they were well hidden.

It was very difficult. The Germans were determined to hold onto every inch of ground. When we captured Naples, we found that the city's water supply system had been destroyed by the Germans, which caused a typhus epidemic among the civilians, and much of the city was placed Off-Limits to occupying G.I. troops. The farmers out in the country began hauling water into the city and selling it for so much per gallon.

Mark Freedom **PAID**

Down The Hatch!

Recollections of the heavenly broth...

One evening Raymond C. "Pop" Hoover, as we were prone to do once in awhile, went out drinking. Most of the night, in fact. He finally decided to sleep it off atop a low stone wall along an Italian road. Came morning, he discovered it was on top of a cliff that dropped into the sea. Good thing he didn't roll over!

Another time, Pop was working in the kitchen. A GI from Texas brought in a case of grapefruit juice, cussing all the time: "What does my family think I need with grapefruit juice?" It was juice okay, Pop and the kitchen crew opened the cans and discovered the contents were joy juice — glorious bourbon. Of course they told the Texan after they'd made sure most of the cans had the quality he'd enjoy.

Back in the Pozzuoli retraining area, Eugene Pirani found a nearby farmer who would sell him homemade cherry brandy, if he'd bring his own bottle. Pirani watched as the farmer filled his bottle, then poured a liter of water into a funnel at the barrel's top. He just shrugged and explained that this barrel was all he had, and since it would have to supply thirsty GIs and himself until the war ended, he naturally had to keep on diluting it. Pirani was happy he'd gotten there early!

And then there was the "D" Company replacement at Anzio, from Gravel Switch, Kentucky. He could read but not write, but his education had included things that mattered. He found a copper coil from a knocked-out German vehicle, punched a hole atop a jerrycan, begged enough flour from the cooks to make a pressure-proof seal, and made an eye-watering potion from fig bars contributed from his buddies' rations. If you held your nose real tight and closed your eyes, you could swallow his Anzio lightnin'.

Rome
Cisterna
Anzio
TO FRANCE
Cassino
Venafro
Chiunzi Pass
Minturno
Pozzuoli
Naples
Salerno
ITALY
SICILY
Sciacca
Gela
N
Mediterranian Sea
83G INVASION ROUTES

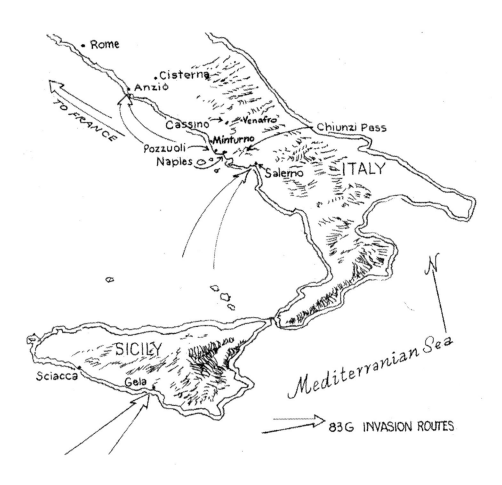

Volturno River Crossing

William C. Ford:

Once we had cleared the enemy and all their snipers from Naples, we continued toward the Volturno River. Up until this time the weather had been hot and dry. But suddenly now the rains began, and it poured continuously. What had been thick dust in roads and fields turned to deep mud in only one night. The rain flooded streams and drainage ditches, making it very difficult for us to move, but we continued to struggle and fight our way to the Volturno River.

The Germans had set up a strong, natural defense line at the River, and were determined to hold there. The Volturno was flooding over its banks, and would have been difficult to cross even under normal conditions. Now the flooding made it a real problem.

We set up our mortars and began laying a smoke screen for the British Royal Engineers who were building a bridge across the river. The German 88mm and larger artillery continuously shelled the bridge and our mortar position.

Due to the wet, soft mud, our mortar baseplates were sinking deep into the ground. We put rocks and timbers beneath them to help keep the baseplates from sinking so fast. Soon our own Artillery also began firing smoke shells, helping us to maintain a smoke screen for the Engineers.

The Engineers finished the pontoon bridge at night, after our 16-hour mission of laying smoke continuously. We then continued laying smoke as the tanks crossed the bridge to support the Rifle Companies.

After having crossed the Volturno River and moving about ten miles north, we pulled out of the lines in the middle of October and moved back to Amalfi to re-equip and get some much needed rest.

"I grabbed the hot barrel by myself... and was the first one back at the truck."

Venafro

Bill Gallagher:
We moved into a position at Venafro to support two Ranger Companies. We established an OP high on a mountain, observing German movements, and brought up water and rations each night.

One day we spotted two figures moving across a field, running. I said to George Tyma, who was connecting telephone communication, "Who do you think they are?"

Close by, a Ranger officer overheard me, and said "Let them come closer."

We held our fire, and when they drew somewhat closer, one of the Rangers raised his rifle and fired a shot over their heads. The must have heard the zip of the round just over their scalps, because they immediately raised their arms. We motioned for them to come forward, and the Ranger officer told Tyma and me to escort the two prisoners down the mountain to a certain cave, where we'd find Captain Sam and Ranger Colonel Darby.

When we arrived at the cave, Darby met us and said, "Well, what do we have here?" I said "They seem to be saying they escaped from Jerry. They're Italians who were forced to work for them." Whereupon Darby said "Take them further down the mountain to the kitchen. Tell someone to feed them, then bring them back up here."

Well, Tyma and I liked this idea because the Rangers ate in style. We chowed down, and returned to the cave with the Italians. Darby had a GI who spoke Italian with them, and the two guys really opened up, telling Darby where big guns were, different German field positions, and what have you.

The Colonel gave us permission to leave, and rejoin our Company. So, up the mountain we went to do some more observing. But the food...ah! That was great!

Wofford L. Jackson:
At Venafro it rained all the time. If the powder rings got wet we would fire shorts, and the only way we could prevent firing dangerously short was to make sure we only used dry powder. When powder rings got wet or even damp, we would strip them off the shells. We occupied this same position for weeks, and had piles of powder rings in the mud around our mortars. One day a civilian

expert came up to our position. He had been sent over from the States to figure out why we were using so much more powder than shells. He said "Uh-uh — I see why!" He ordered us to pick up the muddy rings, and said they had to be conserved. We told him in a very ugly way to get the hell off the mountain. The next day he came back with men from Headquarters Company with large sacks and they picked every one of them up. I don't know for sure what they did with them. We heard they strung them up on strings in a large cave to dry out. Somehow the cave exploded. We never heard of that civilian expert again.

Reno Toniolo:

One night at Venafro we packed up four mortars with ten rounds each, and went to our left flank by trucks and set up to fire at something we were too close to, for us to stay there. Under cover of darkness we set up to fire ten rounds each. The gunner lowered the elevation wheel after each round. The enemy could see the flashes of our mortars, and we had to get out of there. The four squads fired all forty rounds as fast as we could.

The trucks were waiting for us about a half-mile down the road. We had taken wet sandbags with us to put around the hot barrels. The plan was for two men to carry the barrel, two the baseplate, and one the unipod. I grabbed the hot barrel by myself with the wet sandbags, and I was the first one back at the truck. Needless to say, the Germans plastered that area just after we were gone. Never before, nor any time after that, had we fired that many rounds so fast!

Sam Bundy:

Arriving at Venafro late at night, we set up at the foot of Graveyard Hill. Scheduled fire, day and night. Kitchen moved up with us and served two hot meals a day.

It rained hard, day after day, and with the deep mud, was a terrible mess. Shelling was bad. A few hit in our area, and wounded several men. Sergeant Joe Jones wounded and sent to hospital.

At one time in Venafro, an alternate position was set up some hundred yards away, and it was used for night firing. We moved in, fired, removed barrels and evacuated the position. (Hit and run firing). 35 days were spent here under constant enemy fire, and air attacks. We expended approximately 10,000 rounds of ammo here.

Andrew C. Leech:

Our troops had just taken Venafro, a short distance southeast of Cassino, so we moved into the town, which was shelled and bombed to pieces.

I ran into a Ranger and asked him if there were still snipers in the town, and he said "Yes, we just killed six down the street!" We loaded up into trucks and wound around to the outskirts of the town to an olive grove, and dug in for the night.

The next morning we were awakened by Jerry planes bombing our forward positions, and we heard machine guns up on the mountain above us. We noticed Jerries all over the tops of the peaks. Our "C" and "D" Companies opened up on them, trying to chase them off the mountain.

We moved out, and marched up to the center of the mountain, which was in the shape of a horseshoe, and went into position. We were almost surrounded by the enemy, with only one way of escape. The Jerries up there could observe us from all sides.

The Rangers started attacking up the high hills ahead of us. It was really tough for them going uphill under mortar and machine gun fire. The Jerries would launch a counterattack and push the Rangers down. We shot our mortars so fast we melted the firing pins on some of them, and almost melted the barrels. We would succeed in driving them back and the Rangers would take the hill, but during the night the Jerries would retake it. Many times the Rangers passed by and patted our mortars, and some even kissed them, stating that they had saved their lives.

The Jerries threw shells all around us. They started pouring them in on our ammo dump and set it on fire. Shrapnel was flying everywhere. The smoke from the White Phosphorus was so dense we were forced out of our holes and we ran down the road as the shrapnel from our own shells whizzed all about us. Finally we found a culvert, so in we went to await darkness before venturing out again.

In the meantime the Germans began shelling our gun positions and set the ammunition that was around them on fire. This gave our boys an awful beating and wounded several men.

We had only a small amount of ammunition left and the Jerries were zeroing in on us and could fire on us at will, so there was only one thing left for us to do. That was to fire our remaining ammunition and get out. That we did, and under cover of darkness we pulled out.

We got a day or so of rest, and then came back up by night, and set in a new position which was at the foot of a steep bluff.

The Jerries held the high peaks above us, but they couldn't shoot over the cliffs at us with anything but mortars, so we started giving them the works. We were well dug in and so hard to get at, the Jerries could not move us.

We sent out and got some pack mules to bring our ammunition up the mountainside. Our boys had trouble with the mules because they couldn't comprehend our language. We then sent out and got Italian ex-soldiers to drive them for us.

We stayed in this position about a month and took some awful beatings. Once a shell landed near a gun position and injured a whole squad. One Lieutenant and our Communication Sergeant were blown up by land mines. A squad Sergeant was hit by shrapnel and killed.

I was way out in front of the Company with my BAR on security day and night, living in a foxhole where you couldn't show yourself, and it rained most of the time. Mud was about ankle deep in my foxhole, and it was some cold. My assistant went down one morning on sick call and was killed on his way down.

We finally were relieved and we sure did need it for we were all shell shocked and worn out.

Reno Toniolo

We were set up in an olive grove at Venafro for 36 days, wet every day. I never saw so much rain. Chuck Carullo had an uncle somewhere in Italy, but didn't know where. On the 36th day we were sent back to somewhere near Sorrento for training to hit Anzio. While there, Chuck got the address of his uncle. Guess what. Chuck's uncle owned the olive grove that had been our position for 36 days! That explained why, when Chuck would walk along the road back then, Italians he'd meet would say to him "You must be related to so-and-so because you look so much like that person", but Chuck just hadn't put it together.

In that same olive grove, I was to post two men at guard on our left flank. It was very, very dark and raining as usual. I took them out there by myself, dumb dumb thing that I did. The place was terraced with stone walls about four feet high. I walked straight off one of those walls. Could have broken my back, leg, or whatever!

Minturno

Lee Steedle:

My first night in combat as a "D" Company replacement, we moved into a position near Minturno. Some of us had been assigned to man the machine-gun, two at a time, at two-hour intervals during the rainy night. When my turn came, one of the other new replacements, thinking I had stayed in my water-filled hole, walked to its edge to awaken me. I had been fast asleep on the level ground two feet away. I saw a huge yellow flash through my closed eyelids, as concussion lifted me off the ground. The man, whose name I'd barely gotten to know, had stepped on an S-mine — a Bouncing Betty. It had been propelled about three feet into the air by a small charge, and exploded as an air burst. Since I was lying almost directly under the explosion, most of the shrapnel had blown outward rather than down, luckily only wounding me in one leg and shattering the stock of my carbine. The other man wasn't so lucky. There wasn't much the medics could do for him.

Our angry officers complained bitterly to infantry battalion headquarters when, after Engineers had again swept our position, another S-mine was discovered very close to where one of our squads had set up the night before.

Robert F. Thorpe:

I joined Hq. Company in March, when we went to Minturno. We slept in a minefield that was not completely cleared.

An S-mine popped out of the ground while we were laying telephone line. Later one killed a Lieutenant from Pittsburgh, and a Private. It also took an arm from a Sergeant. I was about 50 feet away from that one.

Raymond (Pop) Hoover:

Somewhere after Venafro "C" Company was relieved for a few days rest. We arrived after dark, and set up our pup tents. Three days later when we were ordered to move up again and were tearing down, I couldn't believe my eyes — under one corner of my blankets I found a land mine!

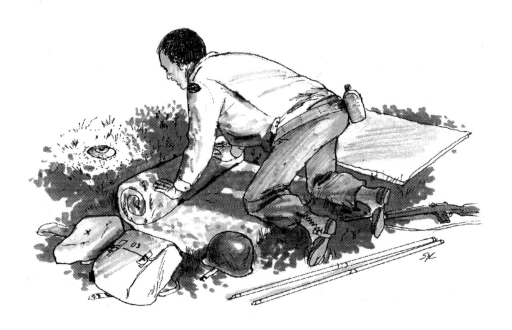

"Under one corner of my blankets I found a land mine!"

Bill Gallagher:

I found myself one day observing in a tower in the mountains of Italy with Lieutenant Walter Hauser. Jerries began shelling close, and maybe had seen us. I said "Let's get the hell outta here!" Hauser was on his hands and knees, searching for something. I was ready to flee this position, and there he was, looking for a pencil he had dropped, a momento from his father imprinted with the logo of the company where he was employed. I cried again: "To HELL with that, Lieutenant, let's get outta here!"

We finally made our way down a winding staircase, then crossed a bridge, when the Germans made two direct hits on the OP tower we'd just left.

When the 88 barrage lifted, we went back to see if we could still retain that high point as an OP. Then we noticed for the first time that the tower windmill had been built in Chicago. So here we were in Italy, using a Chicago OP!

Even when I became a squad leader, Hauser took me with him to OP's. I guess both being Philadelphians, we had a lot in common!

"To HELL with that, Lieutenant, let's get outta here!"

"Hell On Earth" — The Anzio Beachhead

William C. Ford:

Our advance beyond Venafro stalled at the Germans' mountainous Gustav line anchored at Cassino. We were pulled off the line from Venafro to make an assault landing at Anzio, on the west coast of Italy south of Rome. Designated Operation Shingle, this amphibious landing was intended to cut the German supply and communications and to outflank their Gustav line.

A Ranger task force of the 1st, 3rd, and 4th Ranger Battalions, the 509th Parachute Battalion, and 83rd Companies "A" and "B" landed on the beach at Anzio at 0200 hours, January 22nd, 1944. The landing caught the Germans by surprise, and met almost no resistance during the first hours ashore.

Morton Gorowsky:

About 4:00 a.m. we loaded onto DUKWs from our LST and headed for the beach. I hoped this time not to get my feet wet. We got ashore in support of Darby's Rangers, and it seemed to be a breeze. We set up in position and soon heard a rumor that the Rangers were only 10 miles from Rome.

...maybe it was not going to be as peaceful as it seemed at first.

I was loading sandbags to keep the baseplate from moving, when Captain Mindrum told a BAR man and me to go to the left flank and dig in, so maybe it was not going to be as peaceful as it seemed at first.

Later the Germans' huge railroad gun that we called Anzio Annie began firing at the harbor. I could see the black smoke when one of those big shells made a direct hit on our supply ship, and it began burning.

I was in Sergeant Kimbrough's squad there until the first week in May. None of us would have believed we'd remain on this small beachhead so long.

Wofford L. Jackson:

A chaplain who survived on Anzio said this: "Surely all who survived the assault on Anzio will go to heaven, they have already served their time in hell". I hope he's right.

We had been at Pozzuoli for awhile, sort of living it up, going into Naples, etc. We took more amphibious training so we knew what the next one would be. We loaded on a British manned LST that had just survived an air attack that night.

Some time before daylight it happened. We had hit a mine. All hell broke loose. I had just been to the toilet and still had my flashlight in my hand. I didn't have a life preserver, but I shined my light on the floor and there was one. It was the CO2 type, with valves so it could be inflated by mouth. I partially blew mine up.

There was one explosion after another. I told my friend Strickland, let's try to get out of here. He said "Oh hell, what's the use". I was a few feet from my pack which had a full quart of Ancient Age 10 year old bourbon in it. I started back to get it. Another explosion and smoke changed my mind. I managed to get to the top deck, where there was pandemonium. Fire started coming from where I had just left. I said poor old Strick.

The deck was strewn with dead, dying, and wounded. The first person I recognized was Frazier. He was really broken up. His foot was behind his neck like a pillow. I had some morphine down below in my pack that I had taken from a medic's pack that had been abandoned on a battlefield. I thought, if I only had that morphine, I'd give Frazier enough to put him out of his misery. I did what I could for him and others.

The deck was briefly lit up from the fire of a hydrogen-filled barrage balloon tied to the ship. I talked briefly with Platoon Sergeant Edward Guinness, and the next minute he was dead. He had grabbed a fire hose and ran to some equipment that was on fire. It exploded and blew him to pieces. A long time later I was able to call his father when I was in New York, and told him how Guinness died. He was a good platoon sergeant — hard, but good.

I thought if there is one more explosion, I'm leaving. It came, and I did. I went off the front of the LST, which is the highest part of the ship. As I hit the water, another man hit me in the back. I thought my back was broken.

I was able to swim around to the side of the ship where there was a group of men. Anything the Army owned that would float was there. I found some wool beany caps and put one on. It felt good. Staff/Sergeant R. M. Fichtler appeared from somewhere. He had a bad wound in one side of his head and face. I tried to get him to put one of the caps on but he refused. I tried to talk to him but he wouldn't talk. All kinds of junk or equipment were being blown overboard. The sea was rough. Somehow I must have got in a current, and soon I didn't see the ship anymore. I would see another man once in a while. Most were about to give up. It was cold and rough and dark.

I heard a man hollering "Lord save me!" over and over again. When I got to him it was our last Platoon Sergeant, Staff/Sergeant Max E. Nestler. I got behind him and grabbed him by his shirt collar and tried to talk to him. He never would say anything but "Lord save me!" I held him from floundering under until my left arm got numb. He was hollering as he went under.

I talked to other men who were rational. Some said "I just can't stay any longer", and then would go under. It would have felt so good just to give up. If you have been so sleepy in church or some other meeting that you could hardly stand it — that's the way it was. But I knew I had to fight as long as I could, or I would be gone. You've heard the expression "praying without ceasing". That is what I did.

I saw floodlights off in the distance, and that gave me a little hope.

It was almost dawn, and the sky was just beginning to lighten. I was almost gone when a minesweeper came close, and threw me a rope. I just tipped it with my good hand, and they passed me by. It made me so mad I didn't curse.

I thought, this is going to be rough on my wife and family. I knew that if something didn't happen soon, I was gone. I said as loud as I could: "Lord, Please!" The next moment another minesweeper was beside me with a net hanging down. I said to myself, I'll show what a good man looks like, to those sailors. I tried to go up the net, but could only hold on. Two men came down and dragged me on deck. They had dead men on deck, but one live one: Sergeant Karasuskas. I spoke to him briefly, then I realized I was saved, and I passed out. I could hear them talking but I couldn't move.

I heard one man say "Get a sack ready for this man!" I thought: Oh hell! After all this they're going to put me in a sack and throw me back! But when they started cutting my clothes off, I knew I was saved. Karasuskas died a few minutes later. He could speak about six or seven languages, and shouldn't have been put in a combat outfit.

It doesn't hurt to freeze, but thawing out is a different story. It hurts like hell, and you shake to pieces. When they carried me below decks, the first person I saw was George Young, one of my best drinking buddies. He seemed to be in good shape, and helped me thaw out. We sure did need that bottle of 10 year old Ancient Age!

The Germans had plenty of air power. They bombed and strafed us constantly. When they laid a glider bomb right beside us, we began taking on water. Someone brought me a life preserver. I told him I didn't think I could stand two in one day. The minesweeper YMS3 had picked up eighteen of us, and twelve of us were from the South. Have you ever heard that old country song: "A Country Boy Can Survive"? One of the twelve was Julian McKinnon from Cleo, Alabama. He was a Lieutenant or a Captain at that time. He had saved Dr. DeMarco. The doctor had been "out of his head" since they left the ship. I don't know how McKinnon did it. I'd had an experience with an "out of head" man, and couldn't manage to save him. McKinnon was still looking after him when we were transferred to a bigger ship — another LST.

The first man I saw on the LST was Strickland. I asked him how he got out. He said he didn't know — the first thing he remembered after talking to me was being in the water.

After a few of us survivors from Co. "D" got together, I found out Sergeant Codega had somehow got Frazier off the deck and saved him. Codega got the Soldiers Medal. He should have got the Silver Star.

The Captain of our LST kept asking the Beachmaster to let him unload quickly because we had so many wounded aboard. When we finally unloaded and took off for Naples, that Captain made our LST look like a PT boat.

On the way, Lieutenant Forrester said "Well, Jackson, it looks like you're now a Platoon Sergeant". I said: "The hell I am!" I had just seen all three of our Platoon Sergeants get killed in one day. They would always give me the jobs, but not the rank the jobs called for. I was a Pfc. squad leader through many battles. I'm sure it was because if I didn't have something to drink, I was looking for it. Forrester said: "Okay, now you are a Staff Sergeant, but please go easy on the booze." I didn't promise anything.

Back in Pozzuoli, we got and trained replacements, and went up to a so-called quiet part of the front at Minturno, to sort of break them in. Company "C" ran into a minefield there and lost a few men. After this, we went back to Anzio.

Julian T. McKinnon:

The first light of January 26 revealed a beautiful sight. Through the dawn mist and haze and over the crest of ten to twelve foot waves, we could see a flotilla of Navy ships zig-zagging back and forth in a small area of the Tyrrhenian Sea searching for us survivors who had abandoned a burning LST several hours earlier.

Our Battalion doctor and I had agreed to stay together before we jumped off the LST. The presence of the rescue vessels was not a surprise as we had seen their searchlights in the predawn darkness. Rough seas had made it impossible to hold the beam on the water surface to spot soldiers bobbing in the water. Now it was daylight, we could be seen, and were being hunted.

A single ship headed directly toward us. We had been spotted by the crew of YMS 3 (Yard Mine Sweeper). A sailor on the bow threw a life ring which we grabbed. Instantaneously, the sailors on the deck were yelling to us that they had not held the line attached to the life ring, but they would be back. After the next life ring toss we were pulled to a chain ladder with wood rungs hanging midship port side.

We had had experiences with these hard to climb ladders while participating a year earlier in amphibious training in North Africa. YMS 3 was rolling 37 degrees when we grabbed the ladder as the ship rolled toward us. The roll to starboard lifted us out of the water but without enough strength to hold on to the ladder, we fell back into the sea. The second attempt at the ladder produced the same results. The Navy took command. On the third attempt several sailors came down the ladder and grabbed us as we held the ladder. Safely on the deck, I demanded to be released by the sailors holding me in a vertical position. That was a mistake. I fell face down on the deck. In spite of my excellent physical condition at 22, my body was ready to surrender to the Navy's care. Stripped of my cold, wet uniform, I donned Navy long woolen underwear, and wrapped in wool blankets I drank a glass of brandy. The ordeal was over, except when I later learned how few of our buddies had been so lucky.

After several hours sleep we went up on deck. It was a beautiful day, the seas had calmed and the sun was shining. That afternoon we transferred to a LST for the return trip to Naples. After training new replacements we rejoined the 83rd at Anzio for the eventual push toward Rome.

William C. Ford:

"C" and "D" Companies were to follow-up after the initial landing, to support and reinforce. We were on LST 544, a lend-lease ship manned by British sailors. Our LST was loaded to capacity with tanks, trucks, jeeps and half-tracks, all loaded with ammunition and loaded with 5-gallon cans of gasoline. We were on the top deck, and were to go ashore first on January 26th. We were just waiting for orders to go ashore. It was raining and sleeting, with some snow. It was very cold. We were doing our best to stay dry and warm. About 2:00 a.m. the LST was hit on the starboard side by a floating mine. The powerful explosion knocked out the communication system. We did not receive any orders to abandon ship because the system had been destroyed.

As the explosions and fires continued to spread, ammunition and trucks began to explode and burn. It was terrible — explosions blew many men off the ship. Many were killed.

We knew we had to get off the LST, so we lowered a rope ladder off the port side. The ladder didn't reach all the way to the water, so when we reached the bottom, we dropped off into the sea. The water was very cold and the waves were high. I was trying to stay away from fuel burning on the water's surface. I remembered what I had been taught in amphibious training in Africa — to force my way away from the ship. So I put my foot against the hull and pushed myself away from the sinking LST.

It was impossible to swim, even though I had a life belt. The waves would roll me over and over as they came along. As I got further away from the LST I could see men everywhere, and most of them were dead. The Germans had been bombing our convoy and dropping sea mines earlier, and we must have hit one of these. The tide was going out, and soon I could no longer see the burning LST.

As the rough waves continued to beat against my body, I was swallowing more salt water, and was getting weak. I was trying to stay alive, but I thought about giving up and not fighting any longer. Then I thought about my father and mother and brothers and sisters, and continued to fight for my life. I could almost see my mother's and father's faces.

I was full of salt water and passed out, I don't know for how long. I went so far out into eternity, I saw something Great out there. I cannot describe what I saw at this time. I no longer had any pain or suffering from the cold and the huge waves. Suddenly I realized I had to return. Nobody was making me return, I had to return. I regained consciousness and began to suffer again. Then I saw a ship working its way toward me. The sailors threw me a rope, but I was too weak to hold on. But I saw a loop in the rope, put my arm through it, and pressed the rope against my body. The sailors pulled me very slowly toward the ship. They had lowered a rope ladder, and two of them

"Impossible to swim... waves would roll me over"

climbed down to the bottom. They each reached one of my arms, and carried me up the ladder to the deck where I passed out again. The first words I heard then, since leaving the LST were "Good soldier, spit up all that salt water!"

Later I was lying on a bunkbed, covered with warm blankets and drinking coffee when the ship's Captain, John Ross, came and asked me questions. He had thought I was a pilot who had been shot down, because they'd found me all alone in the sea. But when he saw my Army uniform and heard about the LST sinking, he could not believe I had survived the cold water and waves for six long hours.

Captain John Ross told me that I was a long way from Anzio, and that his ship was the USS Pilot Fleet, and that their mission was chasing submarines, and that they would stay out sixty days hunting subs before they could return to Naples. I must have lost my memory for about twenty days. I don't remember the part about returning to Naples or getting back to the 83rd in Pozzuoli. I could not remember what my mother and daddy and brothers and sisters looked like. I wrote home and asked them to send me a picture of them. Once I began receiving pictures and letters from home, my memory began to come back . I don't remember leaving the sub chaser, or whether I thanked the sailors for saving my life.

Raymond (Pop) Hoover:

I remember very little about being wounded during our LST disaster. I only recall coming up from a lower deck, and having my helmet blown off by an explosion, probably from the ammunition that was then blowing up on the top deck. All I know after that is that a friend of mine in the 45th Division, found my body toe-tagged later on the beach, and then wrote my mother that he had seen me dead. Luckily though, my mother received word from the government saying that I was alive and in the hospital, the day before my friend's letter of sympathy was delivered to her.

Edward L. Trey:

When our LST 544 hit a mine early on January 26th, the fierce conflagration resembled a volcanic eruption. I donned a gas mask as dense smoke filled our disintegrating vessel. The total loss of ship's power prevented lowering the life rafts, but I managed to loosen several rafts by severing their cables with my trench knife. Conflagration amidship prevented my traversing to the bow, but I donned a life preserver and was able to help lower one individual down the ship's anchor cable, where we held on awhile. A short time later, he disappeared beneath the rough waves.

I had it in mind to swim to Sardinia, not knowing where Sardinia was. After many hours of bobbing in the cold water, numbness and a sense of futility settled over me. I called on my Maker for mercy, and it seemed to me that I heard a voice saying "We are not ready for you yet!"

Some time later, along came a British LST. The crew hung a ladder over their side, and while I held on, the ladder was raised, bringing me to their deck. Some hours later, while swathed in blankets and warmed by liberal doses of Scotch, a crew member told me they'd had their deck gun zeroed on me in the water, thinking that the dark blob of my body was a mine. I must have come very close to being blown to bits. The next morning while on top deck, I spotted a Stuka dive bomber making a torpedo run on us. I yelled to the gun crew, who blew the Stuka apart with a direct hit.

When I was debriefed by a ship's officer, I stated that the Captain was observed leaving his ship before I did.

A short time after this, I was deposited safely on shore at Anzio, and was taken excellent care of by the gun crew of a British 25-pounder. When I felt a bit more recovered, I trudged off in search of the 83rd. I arrived back at our outfit just in time for the welcome of a German butterfly bomb shower.

George R. Borkhuis:
The trip by LST from Pozzuoli, near Naples, to Anzio Beach below Rome, was uneventful until we arrived off the coast of Anzio. It was raining, hailing, and the wind caused high waves which made walking on the deck hazardous. The LST was manned by an Irish crew with a very tough Captain who anchored the ship awaiting further orders to unload. We could see fires burning on the beach.

The driver of my mess truck said he was cold and was going below to get warm and get a few winks of sleep. I stayed under a tarp in the rear of the truck. I had just about fallen asleep when there was a terrific explosion and crash. I opened the tarp and saw flames coming out of the elevator shaft right alongside of my truck.

I jumped to the deck and saw Sergeant Nestler. Together we grabbed a fire hose to put out the fire, not realizing there wouldn't be any water pressure. We left the hose, and he said he was going to find some way of getting off the ship. As the ship started to list, I slid toward the port side.

Upon reaching the rail, I started to think, "I can't swim, but I also don't want to burn to death, what shall I do?" I figured drowning would be easier. I found a rope fastened to the rail, grabbed it and slid into the water. I kicked against the side of the ship as I was afraid of being sucked into the propellers, again forgetting that the ship had no power.

My head hit something hard and I reached out to find it was a gas can. I held on to the handle and at about the same time, two GIs and a British sailor held on too. We floated alongside the ship and at one point an ambulance rolled off the sloping deck and splashed into the sea a few yards ahead of us. We floated for awhile. Dead silence! I turned to face the two GIs and saw that they had frozen to death; they had obeyed Army rules and had removed their clothing before entering the water, while I had everything on, overcoat and all, except the helmet. I then checked the British sailor who was wearing a Mae West jacket, and found he too was dead.

Now I was scared! Alone in the sea, twenty foot waves, rain, hail, and freezing cold. Gradually the LST passed out of sight. It was pitch dark and the hail beat on the can like a drum at a state funeral. At one point I imagined I saw my whole life pass before me like a motion picture, the good and the bad. I had heard that just before one dies this sometimes happens. I then said my prayers and got ready for the end. Dawn was breaking by this time.

Suddenly I was lifted on a wave and thought I saw a ship in the distance. I did! I tried to wave with my free hand, but the ship turned away from my view. Later I saw another ship, again I waved and thought I heard a voice. The ship seemed to stop moving, but gradually it came nearer. Then I heard a voice saying "Hold on, we see you!" When they were a few yards away, a life ring was thrown to me. My free hand was so frozen I couldn't grab it. A sailor tied a rope around himself and jumped overboard. He swam to me, grabbed my coat collar, and pulled me to the side of the ship. "Are you okay?" I said "I'm okay", and that's all I remember.

When I came to, I was on a deck with crew members pumping my chest. Then I was given some black coffee, and after drinking it I must have thrown up the whole ocean! I was then given a good cup of coffee. I drank it and then was helped down into the crew's quarters. The chef had a pancake breakfast ready, but I couldn't eat it.

I then found out that the ship was an American sub chaser, and couldn't carry us very long because they were on duty. I was

"...an ambulance splashed into the sea a few yards ahead of us."

transferred to an American minesweeper that was scheduled to return to Naples. Again the chef had breakfast ready, and this time I ate heartily. I was only on the ship about an hour when I was transferred to an American LST in Anzio harbor. It was going back to Naples and I was going with it. While I was waiting, a small ship came alongside and there was a lot of commotion. It left in about twenty minutes, and our Captain told us that there were some members of the mined LST taken aboard.

We finally left Anzio that evening and arrived in Naples in the next morning. I was placed in a building formerly used by German officers. It was called "The Survivors House". There were six of us, myself and five of the minesweeper crew that had tried to rescue us, but had been hit by a mine themselves, together with a dog that had been badly burned. We were treated for white phosphorus burns and eventually released.

I managed to hitch-hike to Pozzuoli where our outfit was stationed for refitting. After replacements came in and were trained, we all returned to combat near Cassino.

*Mark Freedom **PAID***

They Could Read Our Dog Tags

Because the Anzio landing had caught the Germans by surprise, resistance had at first been light. Beachhead forces moved inland several miles, but the Germans held the hills in an arc surrounding the plain of Anzio, and brought in strong reinforcements from their Gustav Line reserve units. On January 29th the lst and 3rd Ranger Battalions launched an attack on Cisterna, with their 4th Battalion in ready reserve. Companies "A" and "B" of the 83rd fired in support of the Cisterna attack.

Andrew J. Connolly:

The night the Rangers attacked Cisterna, the sky was full of flares and tracers. Theirs was to have been a surprise attack, but the Germans had been waiting for them. The Rangers occupied buildings inside the town, and were surrounded. When daylight came, our "A" Company was firing continuously in support of the Rangers and of our "B" Company that had moved into the line as infantrymen rather than mortarmen. We got word that the 4th Ranger Battalion had escaped, but went back in, and were mostly wiped out. The following day we did no firing, we were told the Rangers had been lost. When we got to Cisterna months later, we saw all the German foxholes. The Rangers had been destroyed by an overwhelming force.

Our lst and 2nd platoons of "A" Company dug into the banks of the Mussolini Canal to be ready to support "B" Company who had formed a defensive infantry position. Across the open field came Lieutenant Colonel Hutchinson to check how we were doing. All was well until the Colonel left, then we took a shelling from the Jerries for quite a while. We could have done without the visit.

Sam Bundy:

Sunday. Moved up to support a Ranger attack on Cisterna di Littoria. First platoon set up along road, and fired 204 rounds of HE and 47 WP. In evening set up to support "B" Company, which had gone ahead to form a defensive infantry position. Fired upon enemy and laid a smoke screen, but by late afternoon a counterattack was staged, and we fired upon enemy infantry. We received orders to stay in our present position, dug into banks of Mussolini Canal, for defensive purposes. Rangers are trapped in Cisterna, practically given up as lost.

February 18th diary entry: First platoon was taken under small arms fire, was forced to destroy one mortar several hundred yards ahead of their CP. Another mortar except for barrel was left. First Sergeant Kenney fired First Platoon upon enemy infantry, and for remainder of day on infantry and tank advances. Repulsed numerous tank advances and pinned down and repelled infantry assaults. Among targets fired upon were six M6 tanks — fire directed by Sergeant Kennedy from an OP under direct fire from M6 tanks.

WP was fired on infantry entrenched in canal position — effective. To add to discomfort of being fired upon by tanks, planes strafed and bombed nearby. An anti-tank gun emplacement close by our OP fired upon six tanks, disabling one. The remaining five fired back and scored a direct hit on the AT emplacement, ammo exploded, and it seemed all hell broke loose. Incessant volleys of artillery shells, all night, going in both directions.

One volley fell into Company Headquarters and 2nd Platoon areas. Colonel Darby, whose Rangers had been wiped out, now commands 179th Infantry.

Andrew C. Leech:

The 3rd Infantry Division had caught up with us and was making a daylight attack. We saw them coming all spread out in battle formation — crouched and ready for action. They were as calm as could be, laden with packs and equipment. Their faces showed signs of weariness, but very determined they marched out across the open plain in broad daylight, braving artillery and small arms fire. They marched right into enemy territory and dealt with the enemy in their foxholes and pillboxes. It takes men with guts to walk face on into death and see men die and to fall by their side in agony all along the way. May they not have died in vain!

I later looked into some Jerry foxholes, and some of them lay with guns still in their hands. One machine gunner still grasped his machine gun, but he had been drilled through the eye. He was a lad of only about 18. Some of us were detailed to collect these dead at night and bring them back to a collection point to be buried.

We were caught in a tank battle. The Germans threw their artillery at us, as they could reach any point on the beachhead.

We next pulled back up to the edge of the coast and set up a defensive position there. We spent about a week here with headquarters being in an Italian home. We slept all about the house and some in haystacks and others in the doghouse, barn and anywhere available. We were shelled and bombed constantly.

While here our planes came to our rescue. We looked up one morning and saw hundreds of bombers coming over us wave after wave. We watched them drop their bombs. Clouds of flak went up at them. Usually one or two would be knocked down out of each wave, and we watched the crew to see what happened. Some jumped and were captured. Some of them jumped from their planes only to have them explode and catch their chutes on fire. Some managed to get back across the line before bailing out. But nevertheless, they accomplished their mission and softened the Jerries up for us in a time of need.

Next we moved back over on the British sector near the Factory area and set up. It was here that the Jerries warned us that they would give us five days to surrender or be pushed into the sea.

We held fast, but sure enough they threw a large scale attack against us. They had told their men that we were evacuating and that they were coming in to mop up. They came riding at us in Tiger tanks. We were forced to give some ground, but we had some tanks dug in with their turrets sticking out. They ran into these and were mowed down. Then on came the foot troopers shouting and running recklessly into death. We did a good job of mowing them down and stopping the advance, so I guess they changed their minds about us evacuating.

Night firing mission at Anzio.

59

The Factory area changed hands three times in one day. We were forced out of our position and withdrew to a new one about a half mile back. Here we set up headquarters in an old abandoned house. The next morning a plane spotted us and attacked the house. The German pilot made a direct hit on the house and killed one of our lieutenants and a jeep driver. Several others were wounded.

I had just walked out of the house, and was in a foxhole nearby. His explosives almost knocked me out for a minute, and I came to, to find that the bombs had set off one of our ammunition piles nearby, and shrapnel was flying all around me. I knew I had to get out of there so I crawled to a chicken house where there were two jeeps parked nearby which had been hit by shrapnel and were burning.

Later, I ran into the house and it was a wreck. There lay the bodies of two comrades. Three others had been carried to the hospital. The men that were left had run across the road to some scrubby bushes. Meanwhile the Germans had seen fires burning there and began to shell the place, so I knew it was time to get out. I ran across the road just as another German plane caught me out in the open and went into his dive aiming at me. I hit the dirt. There was no cover available so I lay down and raked dirt and sand up over me, hoping to camouflage myself so maybe he would not notice me if he wasn't already shooting at me. As he passed by then I jumped up and ran into the bushes.

We set up back in the woods that night and the ground was so muddy you couldn't dig in without hitting water. We took some limbs and sandbags and built a small trench and lay down after a perilous day. Our mortars were firing salvos about every 15 minutes. The Jerries

Called out of Anzio dugout for firing mission.

knew we were in those woods, so they threw in one barrage after another all night long. We took a beating and had many casualties. One foxhole suffered a direct hit with three of our boys in it. We never found them. Quite a few went to the hospital with shrapnel wounds.

A British group moved up that night and lay down on the open ground in our area to rest until daylight, and boy, were their casualties heavy that night! They were carrying them out on stretchers all night.

We stayed here a couple of nights and I slept in the same foxhole with Claude Kuykendall. We read our Bibles together, said our prayers, and sweated out some hot times while there. The German planes even harassed us by dropping personnel bombs at night. The air raids were frequent here, and we threw up so much flak we had a situation where if the enemy didn't hit you, our own would if you were not under cover.

Frederick W. Endlein:

When we were over on the right flank at Anzio, the veteran outfit we were attached to was relieved, and a new one took their place. Over in a field next to us were a couple of dead cows — you could smell their stink a hundred yards away. A greenhorn lieutenant from the new outfit suggested that we pour some gas on them to burn them up and do away with the smell. This Ninety Day Wonder didn't realize that the Germans were in the hills looking down our throats. We always said they could read our dogtags.

An officer from this same new outfit we were supporting, came over to give us an inspection. He told one man in my squad during the inspection that his rifle barrel was dirty. The GI told him he couldn't get it any cleaner. The officer left to inspect another squad, and in the meantime my GI fired his rifle in the air a couple of times. The officer came running back to find out what was going on. My man told him he was just cleaning his gun.

Wofford L. Jackson:

Anzio was hell on earth. There was no such thing as a rear area. The Germans held the high ground and could see every foot of the beachhead. At the height of the battle we had 105,000 Allied troops on Anzio with our backs to the sea, surrounded on three sides by 120,000 Germans. They had a 280mm railway gun that fired a 550-pound shell. The gun would fire a few rounds, then disappear back into its railroad tunnel. Our planes could never get at it.

If you heard its shell booster you didn't have to worry, it was going over your heads to the beaches or into the harbor. Some men could never resist hitting the dirt every time they heard it. If you didn't hear the booster you wouldn't hit the ground, you would be dead.

I had several sources of getting booze. Some was sent from home. Some was from a still set up in the catacombs in the city of Anzio. Some of our men were involved. Ammo Sergeant Jack L. James from Millington, Tennessee was the instigator, Porter Davis was the consultant. Part of the condenser was made from the recoil mechanism of a 155mm Long Tom. The still was fired with gasoline.

They stole cases of fruit bars and anything else that would ferment. When Sergeant James brought up ammo, if some booze was ready I got my share. Sergeant James lived through the war and then killed himself drinking.

My other booze source was a British soldier named Frank Doren from Coventry, England. Sergeant James was my go-between. I swapped all my cigarettes and candy for all of Doren's liquor ration. One night when James brought up ammo, he said "Jackson, a sad thing happened today. Frank got killed." That really hurt, in more ways than one.

James G. Helsel:

My scariest experience on Anzio was in the position "A" Company stayed in the longest. J.C. Jordan and I were in a hole together. Germans started shelling our area pretty heavy. Once in a while, one of their rounds would be a dud, and instead of an explosion, you could hear it churning through the ground. One of those duds came so close, it sounded like it would come churning right through our foxhole. If it had, I'd probably have died of fright right there. A little break in the shelling came, and Jordan said "I'm leaving here!" I said "Lead, I'll follow!" We ran up to the CP. They had a large bunker built with sandbags. When we went in, my teeth were chattering so fast and loud that First Sergeant Jessop said "Are you typing out the Morning Report Helsel?" I told him "This is not funny — my ass just bit a hole in my underwear!" Within the next two or three days I was washing out some underwear and came across a pair with a tear in the seat. I ran down to the CP and yelled for them all to come out. I then held the underwear up and said "You thought I was bullshitting didn't you!" Jessop never let me forget it.

Reno Toniolo

A few days after the Anzio landing, we had four mortars set up in a swampy, flat place. We could not dig a foxhole because it would fill up right away with water. You had to dig the dirt from the outside and pile it around yourself. At this place I watched two large German planes flying over, with a very small plane to their right rear. I saw the little plane peel off and head right for us. It hit about thirty or forty feet to the right of the First Mortar Squad position, and buried Krutz alive. It made a hole big enough to bury a house in, and it wounded four other men. If it had landed fifty feet more to the left, it would have wiped out our entire platoon of about fifty men. The next day there were all kinds of high brass looking for pieces of the plane, which we later learned was a radio-controlled glider bomb.

One time at Anzio we had moved up too close to fire safely, because the Germans could see our muzzleblasts, and would then lay in heavy fire on us. Also, the Infantry had a .50 calibre machine gun set up next to us, and were firing bursts as harassing fire. Every time they fired, the Jerries would plaster us again. We had to move out of that position. Lieutenant Connolly told me, at the next lull, we're leaving. This was at night, and the password and countersign were: "Ever" "Ready". As we were shagging down the road there were sheep still alive and grazing off to our right. One of the sheep went "Baaaa!" and quickly one of my men yelled "Ready!"

During one of the frequent German air raids, Eppy Danziger was straddled over the slit trench, holding a frying pan over his head. As I ran for cover I asked "What in the world are you doing?" He said "I can't run with my pants down, and my helmet is too far away. At least I have shelter!"

Robert B. Smith:

(From a letter to his wife Annette). I'm now in command of Company "C". It's a good outfit and I know I'll like it. Have the two platoons pretty widely separated and can only go and come at night, so I spend most of my time up with the platoons.

I like the Company fine, and the more I see of these boys the more respect I have for them. The great majority are really just good, brave Americans who want it to be over and to go home. I say they are brave because they are; that doesn't mean that no one is scared, but that they do their job regardless. If I have my way every man (with a very few exceptions) in this Company will get the Bronze Star medal. I think every damn one of them are heroes — the jeep and truck drivers, the communication men, the gun crews, the cooks and all.

The other night my driver and I were going up and ran into a

"The more I see of these boys, the more respect I have for them."

barrage. We hit the ditch and were there about 30 minutes until it was over. When we went up the road a little way we found two of our own linemen checking out the line. They had been in the ditch on the other side of the barrage. It fell between us, and the next time a line is out, out they go again. The driver had to go back by himself. On the way back he was pinned down an hour again, but he takes it as the day's work. They all do.

While I was in the CP we adjusted on a Kraut position. We put in 20 rounds of H.E. The Kraut litter bearers came out waving a white flag and carried off 4 or 6 men. So I guess if killing men is what I'm hired for, I'm at last earning my salt, but I'll be glad when it's over.

John M. Butler:

Dysentery in those days was called "The GIs", and it was a common problem. My most embarrassing memory of the GIs was in Anzio. We were moving up to a point behind the Infantry at dusk. I had the Ammo Crew and a load of sandbags in my truck for mortar emplacements.

Well along the road, the trucks and jeeps stopped. Just at that time Montezuma's Revenge struck. I ran into the field alongside the truck. As it happened I had on a pair of coveralls and they were very difficult to get off in a hurry. Well, I got them about halfway off when I let loose! At the same time the call came to "Move Up!" I had to take off my coveralls and undergarments and run back to my truck; then had to put the soiled clothing up on the winch in front of the truck.

While I was doing that, Captain John McEvoy took one look at me and couldn't believe what he was seeing, which created a lot of laughter among us. My Ammo Crew needless to say, did not want to return to the now stinking truck. YES! This is one of my most memorable memories.

Wofford L. Jackson:

Before we pushed out of Anzio we had to go out in no man's land and dig new positions. We went out after dark and came back in before daylight. One man, Harold Hughes, refused to dig. He was sent back, sent home, and later was Governor of Iowa, and then was a Senator for that State. He always had a drinking problem, but he stunned his supporters after his Senate term ended, by announcing that he was retiring from politics to become a lay preacher and "follow God's calling."

Lee Steedle:

The night of May 22nd, the eve of the Anzio jump-off, our platoon displaced forward, about three hundred yards ahead of our own Infantry outposts, into one of the deep ditches that had drained the malaria-breeding Pontine Marshes making up Anzio's plain. So that we'd be in position to provide fire support at our maximum range as the riflemen attacked, we moved to the forward edge of our own extensive minefield.

Stepping carefully single-file, we followed a line of white tapes that had been pegged to the ground by Engineers who had swept our path some hours earlier. But several other white tapes criss-crossed ours, and at one point First Lieutenant Justin Woomer who was leading us, took a wrong turn that led away from our designated ditch.

The nervous Jerries could hear muffled sounds of movement all along the line. They were expending star-shells suspended by small parachutes at the rate of one every couple of minutes. In that blazing white light we remained upright and still, rather than hitting the ground, to avoid tell-tale movement that would send grazing Jerry machine-gun fire our way. We all knew we were in deep trouble, lost somewhere in no-man's land. But Woomer had been a schoolteacher, and we always found his deep, calm voice reassuring. For sure we were scared, but no one panicked. Finally, barely able to retrace our way to the right marker tape, we dropped into our forward ditch just as the sky began lightening.

...Jerry sniper put a chest-high bullet right between us...

The brightest light came not from the dawn of May 23rd, but from the firing and explosions of tens of thousands of shells, including our own, that converged on Jerry front lines in the minutes before our Infantry climbed out of their holes and moved forward.

By mid-morning we were again able to displace forward along a swept lane through the quarter-mile deep German minefield our riflemen had forced themselves to walk through. Years later, it is still impossible to erase from my mind the terrible cries and human devastation in that bloody German minefield.

Our platoon medic and I got careless and moved around a wall to see ahead, when a Jerry sniper who was probably exulting in having two targets at once, put a chest high bullet between us, as we stood less than two feet apart. With his windage uncertain, the Jerry might have figured he couldn't possibly miss hitting one, if he aimed right between us.

Andrew C. Leech:

When the drive started we were supporting the 1st Armored Division. And on the morning of May 23 all hell broke loose. Our artillery laid down some barrage. Then came the infantry, tanks and mechanized equipment. We broke through and captured the town of Cisterna.

The captured village where the Rangers had been wiped out was a sight to see. It had been shelled for so long. We continued driving. There was no letup once we had broken through their main line. We kept them on the run and didn't give them time to organize and form a new line of resistance.

We were weary as we moved from one position to another and set up and fired a few rounds. The Infantry was advancing so fast they would soon be out of our reach and we would have to move again. We were usually under the fire of German 88's and mortars, and we traveled over all kinds of terrain.

When we gained the heights of the last hill overlooking Rome, we set up our equipment and covered our Infantry as they advanced out across the plain supported by tanks — and on into Rome.

Dale C. Blank:

As everyone who was at Anzio knows, it was sort of a forward rest area for combat troops. All we had to do all day and night was stay out of sight of the German Army, fire our mortars when asked, swear at the tanks when they came up beside our positions to act as artillery, after which they would hightail it to the rear. After everybody got a nice suntan at Anzio someone suggested that we all visit Rome on a holiday and it was positively amazing how the whole Battalion agreed it was a good time to go, since this was the off season anyway. So everybody piled into their personal 6x6 and off we go to see the sights of Rome and maybe be granted an audience with the Pope. The moment we started, we found out the Germans were entirely against the whole idea of us visiting the Eternal City, but after some friendly persuasion and strong argument on our part they came around to our way of thinking.

We were not permitted to visit Rome right away, and had to bivouac on a hill, awaiting our outfit's priority. A Sergeant Pete from another squad was of Italian descent and spoke the language fluently, so he borrowed my .45 Automatic and decided to go into Rome on his own. The night after his return, he gave the weapon back to me with a round in the chamber, with the safety off, and the firearm cocked. I always made sure my weapons were safe at night so as I lay under the mosquito netting, I pulled the weapon from my holster and it promptly discharged a slug about an inch from my wrist. Everybody heard the shot but no one knew where it came from and I wasn't about to tell. From that time until now I have never loaned a weapon to anyone.

The next day we had an incident that didn't turn out as well. About dusk a B-25 bomber came flying over our bivouac area at a very low elevation, so low that we could see the pilot in the cockpit. Nobody was worried, after all it was one of ours. On the second pass over our area, this aircraft dropped a stick of bombs. One man in our Company had sensed something was not quite right, and he manned a .50 calibre machine gun on one of the trucks in the motor pool. The bombs dropped between the dispersed trucks with no direct hits, but shrapnel or concussion killed the man on the machine gun. The trucks took quite a beating. This plane may have been one of ours, but the crew was German. We had word that it was shot down later on another bomb run.

Lee Steedle:

Publicity-hungry General Mark Clark made a triumphal entry into Rome about June 4th, after the Germans had left and had declared Rome an "Open City". This delayed our pursuit, as they must have figured it would. Along with other units, the 83rd was "stacked-up" on surrounding hillsides awaiting road priority.

Figuring that our outfit would remain in its hillside bivouac a couple of days, our platoon medic and I decided to go AWOL and see Rome. We did so, and managed to avoid arrest by MPs who had been detailed to keep GIs out. The Swiss Guards at the Vatican must not yet have been given appropriate orders, because Doc and I walked into St. Peter's with our helmets, and I was carrying my carbine, which a day or two later and forever after, would have been unthinkable. Rome treated us well, and when we got back to "D" Company the next afternoon, happy with what we'd done, and quite certain we'd both be busted down to Private, we didn't care. The great surprise was that neither of us lost our stripes.

Andrew C. Leech:

The next morning we loaded on a motor convoy and started moving through Rome. It took us all day to get through. The people thronged the streets by the thousands, waving and shouting, shaking hands and passing out wine. Photographers were in evidence and cameras clicked as we drove past them. Everybody seemed to be glad, and they had turned out to greet us. Most of the city itself had been spared. It had not been touched by bombs which fell only on the outskirts where the last stand was made.

Sam Bundy:

In wee hours of morning, we continued our truck ride by traveling through Rome. Traffic was so bad that it took us hours to pass through the city. People in pajamas and house coats cheered and applauded, gave wine and whiskey. Irish Nuns said that at last their prayers had been answered. Many pretty well-dressed women.

Wofford L. Jackson:

When we pushed out of that Anzio hell hole, it was like a breath of fresh air. We crossed the Tiber River south of Rome and didn't stop until we reached a place near Tarquinia. We encountered some German bicycle troops. Each one had a bicycle and overcoat. Many of them were captured. It seemed funny to see our infantry riding around on bicycles. The Germans were good at retreating.

We dug-in in this beautiful area, and since a German shell came in occasionally we all dug slit trenches to sleep in. About time we got through digging, word came we had to move. Some Headquarters outfit was taking over our area. I called my platoon together and told them the news. I think the move was ordered on purpose to give those Headquarters people ready-made holes. I told all my men to get into their holes and strain like hell to have a bowel movement and urinate, then cover it a little with a few leaves and twigs. Every man said he was successful. I would have liked to have seen those Headquarters jokers the next day. They couldn't do a thing about our special kind of hospitality.

We stayed in this general area, out of combat longer than ever before. We deserved it too. We made lots of trips into Rome.

One day we got the order to take off all insignia, and that we were going back to Salerno for more amphibious training. We knew that meant a Southern France landing. When we got to Salerno, Axis Sally came on the radio and said "Put your insignia back on.
We know who you are, and the name of every commanding officer in every outfit". So we put our 83rd insignia back on.

Company "D" didn't get started on amphibious retraining. We were told we were going to Ciampino Airport south of Rome near the Tiber River.

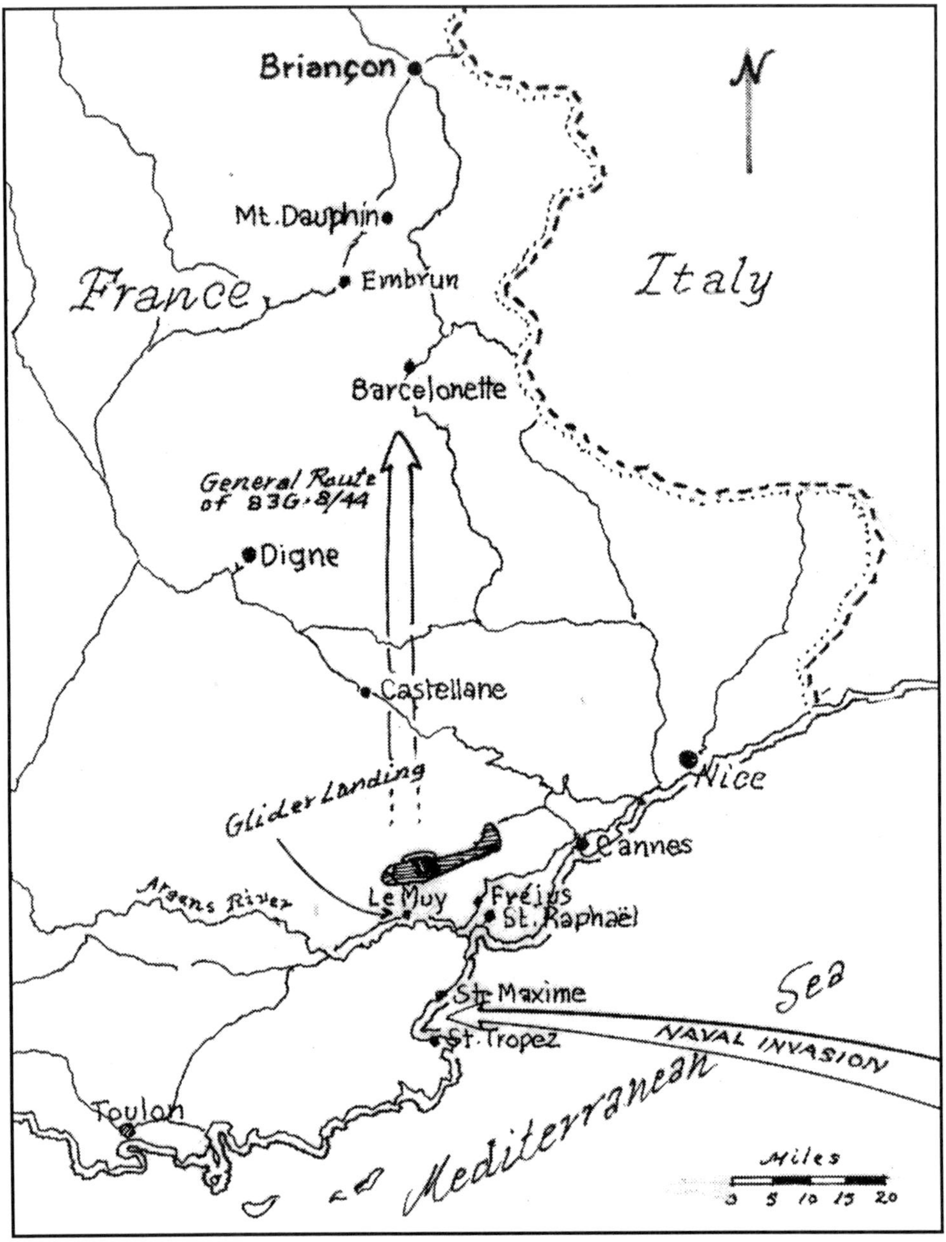
Briançon
N
Mt. Dauphin
Embrun
France
Italy
Barcelonette
General Route of 83G. 8/44
Digne
Castellane
Glider Landing
Nice
Cannes
Argens River
Le Muy
Fréjus
St. Raphaël
Sea
St. Maxime
St. Tropez
NAVAL INVASION
Mediterranean
Toulon
Miles
0 5 10 15 20

Southern France Landings
by Sea and Air

William C. Ford:

We joined together with the 45th, 3rd, and 36th Infantry Divisions, and the 1st Airborne Task Force to make up the VI Corps of the 7th American Army, commanded by Lieutenant General Alexander M. Patch, to conduct Operation Dragoon — the sea and air invasion of Southern France.

By August, 1944 we had already made four amphibious assault landings, two in Sicily and two in Italy. All four had taken place at 0200 Hours on their D-Days. Operation Dragoon however, called for an 0800 hours daylight beach assault; with the airborne units landing some miles inland at dawn. The plan called for our VI Corp to make the initial beach assault.

Samuel Bundy, Jr.:

On July 19th, our drivers left to load jeeps and trucks on ships. We were waiting at an assembly point with the 157th Regiment of the 45th Division. Before dawn on August 5th we were driven by convoy to Bagnoli and loaded on LST 690. Two days later we participated in a dry run landing below Salerno. When this was finished, we returned to Bagnoli, arriving just after midnight, and walked through a heavy smoke screen to our staging area. We were "sealed" in secrecy, and now our diet was mostly "C" Rations.

Perry Rice:

While the 83rd's other three Companies were scheduled to make the August 15th assault by sea, our "D" Company was peeled off to become part of the First Airborne Task Force. Our mission, which we shared with a 75mm cannon company of the Nisei 442nd Combat Team, was to provide fire support for the 517th Parachute Regiment, intercepting German reinforcements at Le Muy, a critical rail and communications point some twenty miles inland.

We pitched our tents near Rome's Ciampino Airport to undergo glider training. The morning we first saw the gliders, we wondered what we had gotten into. They were little more than boxes with wings. Their floors resembled wooden industrial pallets. A blunt front end was hinged to swing upward, high enough to admit either a jeep or trailer. Looking more like bumblebees than the sleek C-47s that towed them, they were perfectly flat-sided, and constructed of doped canvas over rigid pipe frames. These primitive gliders were provided with a combination of small wheels and long skids for landing gear.

At Ciampino we were shown how to lash either a jeep or its trailer with ropes to rings welded to the pipe frames. Three gliders were provided per squad: one with a jeep and two men; another for the trailer with mortar, gunner, and ammo man; and the third carried the rest of the squad with ammo. There were no safety belts: each man tied himself to frame rings with rope, and was taught to inflate his Mae West at the moment of landing to cushion shock from the ropes. We learned to pile and lash the ammo in pyramids, sandwiching W.P. rounds snugly within the H.E., to protect the phosphorus from flak. Our practice landings on Ciampino's runways were deceptively uneventful.

Lee Steedle:

Glider training completed, "D" Company was given a few rest days at Lake Albano, a beautiful, small lake cupped within the Alban Hills between Rome and Anzio. This is the site of the Pope's summer residence, a sort of Camp David retreat from Rome's stifling summer heat. Not wanting us to just loll around, our officers ordered us to set up our mortars one afternoon, to practice rapid-fire into the lake. Two of our men had gone fishing in a rowboat the previous afternoon, and not having caught anything, had tossed in a concussion grenade. This brought a half-dozen fish floating to the surface.

No one was willing to warn the officers, because it would mean getting our two men in trouble. So we fired the shoot — 32 quick-fire rounds, 272 pounds of TNT — into the middle of that beautiful lake.

The next morning the entire shore was lined with dead silver-sided fish. The blazing summer sun did its job, and two days later we pulled out from a stinking Lake Albano. I'm sure if the Pope was there at the time, he wasn't giving "D" Company his blessing.

Wofford L. Jackson;

We went to Rome's Ciampino Airport, near the Tiber River.

We made a few practice landings, tore up a few gliders, and had pretty good times there, going into Rome. I had a good source for cherry brandy near the airport.

The evening before D-Day was hot. Jim Lauro had just been made a Second Lieutenant, and he had just gotten his first liquor ration. He offered me a drink. I turned the bottle up and took me a good one.

Even though I had a good tolerance to alcohol it hit me pretty hard.

I was on my way to get my platoon ready to load aboard, when Captain Lakey saw me. He said "Jackson, come in this tent!" I thought, oh hell, he's going to give me hell for being a little drunk before take-off. I was relieved when he said "How would you like a little drink first?" I said "Just a little one Captain, I want to have a clear head when we land." He was about loaded himself.

One of my jobs was to number the outside of the gliders before take-off. Our two platoon Hq. gliders were numbers 23 and 23J. I was to go in 23J, so I finished the "J" out in letters as big as the side of the glider would hold, spelling out "Jackson" on both sides. We were short an officer, so I was going in as platoon executive and Sergeant Elwood Guthrie was taking my place as platoon sergeant. That changed the seating arrangement. I had to go in number 23, and Lieutenant Perry Rice went in 23-JACKSON instead of me.

We were all loaded and ready to go, when here came the pilot and co-pilot with parachutes hanging off their butts. I said "Fellows, you can't wear those chutes!" The pilot said "We have to, or we can't see out." I said, "Okay, you can sit on them, and that's all." I hadn't shaved in several days, my clothes were dirty, and I knew I looked terrible. One pilot got out a cake his Mother had sent him, and offered me some. He said "You know, my Mother is expecting me home." I said "I may not look like it, but my Mother is expecting me home too! You are still not wearing the chutes, and furthermore we want your flak jackets to put on the floor of the jeep for landmine protection!" They agreed to that.

Fred G. Rand, Jr.:
I joined the 83rd as a replacement Lieutenant in Italy, assigned to Lieutenant Bush's platoon in "A" Company.

The preparations we planned for the beach landing in Southern France included Lieutenant Bush taking one part of the platoon with the mortars, jeeps and other equipment ashore, while I would take the other part. Each of my men was to carry two shells in a backpack as he went ashore. This would insure that we'd have some ammo for initial firing, until regular supplies were offloaded.

While still in Italy, we were given maps that were accurate as to topography and distances, but there was no marking that indicated what country these maps were for. At the time of the planning we did not know if the next landing would be in Western or Southern France, Greece, or where. Bush and I agreed on a spot on the map where the two sections of our platoon would meet after the landing.

On D-Day, August 15th, I and my section were on an LCI, and now had maps identifying Southern France. Lieutenant Bush with the mortars was to land at H+5 hours, and I with ammo at H+7. As our LCI approached the beach, a battleship was firing, causing our LCI to bounce around. At the time, I thought that this might be a much worse landing than expected, since the battleship was still firing at H+7 hours. We went ashore, located the ground area where the two parts of our platoon were to meet, but we could not see any Americans. We stacked the ammo and sat down. Soon a reconnaissance vehicle, mounting a .50 calibre machine gun, rolled up. Men in that vehicle wanted to know what we were doing here. One of our men said something like "We were waiting for you so we could see the show!" Here was I, a new Lieutenant to my men, lost in France with 4.2 ammo, and no mortars to put them into.

Hours later, along come the rest of the platoon with our mortars and jeeps. My men and I were exactly where we were supposed to be, but we had gotten there at H+2 minutes, instead of H+7 hours. It's amazing that with all the dry running and planning we had done in Italy for this operation, we still landed at H+2 minutes instead of H+7 hours. In teaching after the war, I used this as an example of one screw-up that did happen, and wondered how many more had taken place.

William C. Ford:

During the early night hours of August 15th, our planes bombed the beach landing area. Battleships and destroyers lying offshore were firing at the beach with guns and rockets. The long-range barrage lasted until 7:30 a.m., when the destroyers moved close to shore firing point-blank. All was quiet from shore, no answering fire from enemy guns, in this, the St. Tropez/Frejus area.

The 45th Division flagship, the USS Biscayne, received the order to launch Operation Dragoon. As our landing crafts began their run toward the beach, naval guns were still flashing and roaring as large shells whizzed over our heads. Suddenly, as we passed, all guns ceased firing.

Our weather was ideal for an amphibious operation. Experience gained in our previous landings was put to the fullest use. The German 19th Army was defending Southern France, but their opposition was light as we grounded on Red Beach. We moved rapidly across the sand, through barbed wire, and approached a six-foot high sea wall. The Rifle Company ahead of us hurdled over the wall, and we moved our mortars as quickly as possible through a big hole blown out of the sea wall by our big Navy guns. This light opposition was in welcome contrast to the heavy beach fighting we had done at Gela, Salerno and Anzio.

Our first objective was rapidly secured despite some light small-arms and mortar return fire. Later, we encountered large roadblocks with isolated enemy pockets, as we moved along the coastal road toward Ste. Maxime. We finally found heavier enemy resistance at Ste. Maxime, with stiff street fighting that held us up a short time, but we continued to move along the coast road to Plan de La Tour and toward Ste. Aygulf, capturing the high ground south of the Argens River. All coastal roads were cleared of the enemy by nightfall. But the pillboxes and strong points which formed the German defense at Ste. Raphael kept us engaged in fierce fighting. Throughout this first night of our assault we fired constantly on enemy positions. The next day we made contact with the 509th Parachute Regiment.

Perry Rice:

At 2:00 a.m. of D-Day we were awakened and soon lashed ourselves into the gliders we had previously loaded with jeeps, trailers and ammo. I watched as the 100 feet of coiled nylon tow rope unwound and stretched as our C-47 tow plane passed us and picked up speed. Suddenly, like a snapping rubber-band, the rope whipped our glider into the air and we were away. After circling out to sea, it was an awe-inspiring sight to see our vast armada of hundreds of gliders and planes stretching to the horizon. As we passed inland from the French coast we saw ships blazing away at shore installations in the early dawn.

The C-47s cut us loose about 1,000 feet in the air over our Le Muy drop zone at 0700 hours. The Germans had known we were coming, and had loaded all fields in that area with glider traps. These were grids of 15-foot poles spaced in squares, with 5-foot piles of large stones centered in each square. In some fields, they had strung wire between the poles to shear off wings, and in several fields they had suspended fused shells from the wires. But a GI Pathfinder Team had parachuted into Le Muy several days earlier to make contact with the French Forces of the Interior (FFI) partisans. Seeing the condition of the fields, they had radioed warnings and coordinates. This enabled our pilots to come down into fields that had the poles and stone piles, but not the wires and shells. Some pilots chose to crash into other gliders that had just landed seconds before, shearing off other gliders'

The Germans had known we were coming —
they had loaded all fields in that area with glider traps.

wings and tails, but avoiding the deadly poles.

Our own glider wasn't as lucky. After the throbbing speed of a fast
tow, it had momentarily seemed almost peaceful when we cut loose
and circled, as quiet as a bird. Our I.M.G. Corporal Herring and I
were lashed into jump seats behind a jeep trailer. As instructed, we
pulled bolts that sent our big side doors flying away, and the in-
rushing air helped slow our speed. Our pilot and co-pilot, McFarland
and Wilcox, circled, deciding between two fields. Banking steeply to
the right, they saw too late that high-tension wires ran between these
fields. Our lowered right wing was sheared off, and we cart-wheeled
nose-first into the ground.

McFarland was killed outright, with Wilcox and Herring badly hurt
by the loose trailer. I was thrown completely free, and was still
unconscious when Staff/Sergeant Wofford Jackson found me. He later
said he'd wondered if I'd died there, but anyway took time to inject
me with morphine before he had to move the platoon.

Three days later when the sea-borne troops reached Le Muy, I was
evacuated to a Naples base hospital. It took months for internal
injuries to heal, and I wasn't able to rejoin the 83rd until January. At
that, I was lucky. We had only gotten a co-pilot the day before, and
until then I had been scheduled to ride in the co-pilot's seat. It's hard
to imagine that Wilcox would have survived the crash.

Andrew C. Leech:

We landed on the beach near Toulon. The 36th Division landed to our right and ran into plenty of trouble. They lost heavily in the landing. The 3rd Division landed to our left and met light opposition. The advance inland was rapid and we took a lot of prisoners. We ran into a little rear guard action now and then. We were advancing so fast it was a problem keeping supplies up with us. We just followed the roads in convoys until we hit something. Many Jerries were bypassed in the hills, but the French FFI would round them up and bring them in.

These French patriots were a great help to us. They came out with shotguns and knives and led us to where the Germans were hiding and also showed us where the minefields were. They themselves killed many Germans. We saw some with knives rammed through their backs, and it was a sight to see those old grey haired men in civilian clothes so anxious to go along with us.

Wofford L. Jackson:

As we approached our drop zone the C-47 pilots kept trying to get us to cut loose. Our own tow plane was making different engine noises

"I found Lieutenant Rice... gave him some morphine."

and flashing a big red light on top of the plane. I was screaming to cut loose. Our glider pilot finally hit the big latch above the windshield and we were free as a bird. I had a bottle of cherry brandy which I drank on the way. We didn't have a toilet in the glider so I used the empty bottle. At that point I threw it out. As we lost altitude, our pilot got out a map and kept taking valuable time. Our glider seemed as quiet as a mouse as we descended, but the ground was getting closer. I asked our pilot in a quiet, soft voice: "Have you ever heard of the law of gravity?" He then threw the map down and got ready to land.

The Germans had all kinds of glider traps. One was a huge pile of artillery shells with trip wires strung like a spider web. If hit by a glider, the whole pile would explode, killing everything around it. When we were coming in for the landing, the first thing I saw was the wreckage of 23-JACKSON. It and the men were strewn over a wide area. Our glider, and some others, had rough landings and there were injuries, but the only fatalities in our platoon were in glider 23-JACKSON. I found Lieutenant Rice. He seemed to be broken down in his pelvis and was in a lot of pain. I gave him some morphine I'd been carrying, and tried to assure him that help would be on the way. We had to gather up our communication equipment and make contact with the unit we were to support — the 517th Parachute Regiment.

Lee Steedle:

Overall, our airborne landing was successful. Casualties were relatively light and mainly due to injuries caused by jeeps, trailers, and ammo that had been torn loose by landing impact. Some Jerries had put holes in our glider as we came in, but we met no automatic weapon fire while still airborne.

Our radioman lost his arm up at the OP, as we began firing at Jerries holding a crossroad. Resistance was light, but a few hours later a German tank, belly-down, began firing directly into our position. Sergeant Riddle got a paratroop radioman to relay our request to air liaison for help. Luckily, a fighter plane had been circling over Le Muy, and it knocked out the tank in a single pass.

We and the paratroopers had been ordered to take no prisoners before sea-borne troops arrived. Late that first afternoon, a half-dozen Jerries walked into our position weaponless, with hands held high. Not knowing where their weapons might be, we couldn't let them wander loose. Some FFI partisans came along then, a group of about ten men led by a young woman, all armed with light, American-made grease guns. We told them of our "No Prisoners"

We hadn't thought they would kill unarmed prisoners...
we hadn't known the depth of FFI hatred.

order, and the woman said "Don't worry, we'll take care of them for you". The Jerries were then marched away, around a bend in the road, and a couple of minutes later we heard automatic weapons fire. We all hit the ditch, thinking the FFI had run into more Jerries, when along came one of the partisans who said "They tried to escape." We hadn't thought they would kill unarmed prisoners, but until then we hadn't known the depth of FFI hatred.

Robert Sorensen:

We had been in France just a few days. Every day it seemed we, as medics, had to move the aid station forward closer to the front line. I was told to take four medics and supplies up the street in this small town about four city blocks toward the front line, and set up the aid station. The medics always got one of the better buildings that could be curtained off to keep from showing any light at night. In the house I chose, we hung blankets inside the short hallway, and blocked light from reaching the street. The jeep unloaded the four of us along with our medical supplies, and returned for more.

...in stepped two Nazis: SS-Troopers backed up by an SS officer...

We got most things set up for any possible casualties, and were doing odd jobs when the inside curtain blanket parted, and in stepped two Nazis: SS-Troopers backed up by an SS officer, all three with guns pointed at us. Commands and gestures backed us up against a wall in a hurry. I asked Antonio if any of the now four SS Troopers spoke Italian. One did, stating he had spent some time in Italy. Antonio painfully began to talk with this young German.

It was now that I noticed Jacob Miringoff who had been relaxing, was still lying on an opened stretcher on the floor. Our Jewish buddy could speak fluent German, but he was in no position to even speak English. He had been examining a German burp-gun he had "liberated", and had commented that he didn't have any ammo for it, at the moment the SS men had walked into our room. Jacob had quickly pulled a blanket over himself and the burp-gun. Had he risen, the gun would have slipped to the floor.

The four SS-Troopers talked rapidly among themselves. They were scared. One went out to check the street, and then they all left. Now Jacob had understood every word the Germans had been saying. He reported they knew they were in trouble, and debated whether they should stay and be captured or take off down the street as fast as they could? Antonio had told them we were ahead of the Battalion, and suggested they leave immediately or else fight their way back to their own lines. They were ordered by the SS officer to hit the street and go fast.

By this time Jacob could sit up and show us the gun. When I asked why he hadn't talked to the Germans, he replied: "Fat chance that a good looking Jewish boy with a Yiddish German accent and an empty German burp-gun could make any deal with SS-Troopers!"

Wofford L. Jackson:

After a few days we were ordered to help the FFI. The group we came upon were sailors who had scuttled their ship when France surrendered. They were trying to get a very large machine gun up a steep mountain, in order to stop a group of Germans coming across from Northern Italy. We were in the French Alps, above the timber line. The FFI men had only succeeded in moving their heavy gun a few hundred feet, and were ready to quit. They had never seen a jeep. Corporal Strack, my jeep driver, told them he would take their gun up. They didn't believe he could do it. Strack put chains on all four wheels and told them to load it. The machine gun had a large base that had been bolted to the deck of a ship. It just barely fit on the rear floor of our jeep.

Strack told the FFI men to load their ammo and as many men as could get aboard. He gunned the jeep, it went up that steep grade, and they were astounded. We beat the Germans arriving by about thirty minutes. It was a massacre, and the Frenchmen clearly enjoyed it.

Their leader, La Nuufe, was the largest Frenchman I ever saw. He was about 6' 3" tall. He had been a Captain on a warship, and had been captured and tortured. He was mean as hell, and organized this outfit after he escaped.

La Nuufe helped us locate Germans, and we directed fire from our single mortar onto them. The Germans realized there were a few Americans there, but didn't know there were only four of us. Instead of capturing us, we captured some of them. After La Nuufe had interrogated them, and gotten all the information he could, he killed them. Up in those mountains we didn't have much to eat, but plenty to drink, which suited me fine.

We were in the Alps a few miles east of the town of Barcelonette. Company "C" had gone north of us near Briançon. We had it easy compared with them. They were nearly wiped out. Some were captured, along with their mortars and ammo.

A French Morrocan outfit had rescued some of them from the
Germans. These Morrocan native troops were huge men. They were
not black and they were not white. Each one carried a long knife, and
they looked like the character Punjab in the comic strip Little
Orphan Annie.

The Morrocans wanted someone to show them how to use the 4.2
mortars they had recaptured from the Germans. I and a boy who
could speak French — I think his name was Tourmellie agreed to
help them. It wasn't far as the crow flies, but it took a day and a half
to get through the mountains to where the Morrocans had the
mortars. We spent the night at a farm house on the way. They hid our
jeep in a barn, and one of the Morrocans slept there with it. They
were very nice to us — plenty to eat and plenty to drink. We let them
draw a little gas out of our jeep and hoped we'd still have enough
ourselves to get back with.

We arrived about noon at the Morrocans' rear CP. We dropped
Tourmellie off at the mortar position, then I and this French officer
went on to the front. I was lucky, he had been an artillery officer in
World War I. Between the wars he had been a college professor
teaching math. We had a hell of a good time, directing fire and
drinking. We fired at any and everything that moved. We were there
two days.

When we got back to "D" Company, Sergeant Renfroe came to me and
said "Jackson, they are sending us new jeeps, because ours are all
beat up. Please send me back to the medics, I can't take it anymore."
He's the one who gave me the World War I trench knife. In Sicily,
Renfroe was in a ditch, and a German tank ran over him and mashed
his helmet on his head, where he couldn't get it off. We laughed like
hell about that. Anyway, I couldn't refuse. The next day the new jeeps
arrived and he went back.

Renfroe was reclassified, and put in a postal outfit. He wrote that
there were a lot of packages piled up, that couldn't be delivered for
one reason or another. Every few days he would change the address
on one, and send it to me. I had to stop it. I couldn't stand thinking,
this package was sent by some boy's mother, and this boy is probably
dead.

Briançon and Fort Dauphine

Dale C. Blank:

After the Southern France landing Company "C" advanced to the French Alps near the Italian border. We moved into one of the area's old military forts named Fort Dauphine. That was our big mistake, because this was no doubt the most vulnerable and indefensible fort in the entire area. I don't know who made that decision, but it was certainly the wrong one. The entrance to this more than 300 year old fort was too small to get a truck through, so all of our supplies of ammo, food and everything else had to be left in the trucks outside the fort on the narrow and only road.

I set up my .50 calibre machine gun so I could sweep the whole valley looking toward Italy, which was where the German army would come from, if they came. Well, they did come and in sufficient numbers to occupy Fort de Tete which was above and behind us, and which should have been the fort we occupied. All exits to our fort were covered by German rifle and machine gun fire. This meant that after our 4.2 ammo had been expended, we could not get at the additional supplies in the trucks out on the road.

Lieutenant Andre Laus and I destroyed the two mortars that we had in the fort with grenades, after we ran out of ammo. Then Lieutenant Doyle gave me a BAR and a bag of ammo and directed me to go to the back of the fort and he also said he would send a squad of men to follow me. My squad consisted of a Second Lieutenant whose name I don't remember, and a Private Loins from Georgia who always said he was from Texas. The new Lieutenant was pretty good at directing fire. He would give me directions on where the enemy soldiers were, and I would fire a burst from the BAR and then we would move to another spot and do the same thing all over again. Private Loins looked like he was squirrel hunting the way he would calmly look around and squeeze off a shot from his Garrand, then he'd get down and give me a grin like this was a lot of fun. After a while the Lieutenant went back inside the fort and I had to do my own spotting. Well one bag of BAR ammo doesn't last very long, so just about the time the Germans had me figured out and were coming pretty close with some of their shots, I felt something slam into my leg.

Since I was almost out of clips and my leg was starting to hurt, I made tracks for the fort. Happy days, there wasn't a soul in sight anywhere. So I went to the second floor to get some personal belongings and also to have a look at my leg. When I pulled up my pantleg it snagged on something in the wound, so I pulled it out. It looked like a slug that had hit something hard and then hit me. The wound wasn't very deep so I put some sulfa and a bandage on it and went looking for the rest of the troops. I learned later that Lieutenant Laus and Corporal Leonard Hall had been killed by machine gun fire. In 1993 I visited their graves at our National Cemetery in Draguignan, France. It's a very well kept cemetery, but small.

I found the rest of the guys in one of the courtyards. They had already decided we had no chance of getting out of the fort, since we now had nothing left to fight with. Someone found a T-shirt or something white and tied it to a stick and held it up so the Germans could see it, and then we waited. What seemed like a long wait was probably not.

Eventually German soldiers appeared all over the place and lined us up along a high stone wall. There were two machine guns similar to our BARs set on top of the wall directly in front of us, and then we really got scared. The German officer gave a command and all the Germans moved away from us. Everyone in our outfit was certain that we were going to be shot. One man with more faith than the rest of us, Paul Bailey from Nunda, New York, who was with the 45th Division, told us later that he was sure they wouldn't execute us. The Germans had been told to get away from the Americans because we hadn't been searched yet, but not knowing the German language, we didn't know what the officer's order was about. I don't mind telling you that I was about as scared as I have ever been. Being only nineteen years of age at the time, I truly believed I was too young to die.

Shortly we were taken out the back of the fort, past the bodies of the German soldiers we had killed. The bodies were all lying side by side, and the Germans standing there didn't look at all happy with us. Their faces showed how angry they were about their friends being killed.

We were then herded toward Italy, and in a few days we were sitting in the civilian prison in Torino, Italy. The cells were bare except for some straw on the floor which turned out to be our bed. There were five or six of us in each cell.

Robert F. Thorpe:

I went to Company "C" as radio man and forward observer. We went to Briançon. I called fire on Germans and Italians who were clearing a roadblock. Later everything broke loose at the fort. We spotted Germans coming through the woods. I stayed back and fired several rounds at them. When I got back to the road, the jeep was gone, and I made my way back to town under heavy fire. I hid all night in a wood and coal shed behind a house, hearing the screams of the women in town as the patriots were being shot by the Germans.

I was taken prisoner the next afternoon, and taken into Italy, where I spent nine days marching with a group of about thirty German soldiers. I was made to dig my grave by one of their lieutenants when I wouldn't tell him how many ships were in the the invasion of Southern France.

We had marched to Marzabotto, about 20 miles below Bologna, and questioned by a Gestapo agent, and then put into a damp room in the basement. They put me on an all-night train ride to Torino, and I was taken to Gestapo headquarters where the man gave me a hard time for fighting the Germans. I told him the only reason I was there was because I believed in freedom and liberty. With that, he went back into his office and slammed the door. After that, I joined the rest of the guys at Torino prison.

Lloyd L. Fiscus:

As we entered Briançon on August 28th, we were greeted by men of the 180th Infantry Regiment, 45th Division. We were to relieve them and set up a defensive position in Fort Dauphine, one of the five medieval forts, high on an Alp mountainside. The scenery was beautiful, with the sun shining on snow-covered peaks. When we met the soldiers we were to replace, they told us of the fresh eggs available and of the beautiful girls in the town. They said we would be taking over the chosen land. "Chosen Land", Hell! We never did get to eat any eggs or see any women.

As we were setting up our mortars and positions in the fort, we saw movements around the area. We were told that it was the Free French troops scouting the hills. It was a quiet night and I had been on outpost guard from 3:00 to 6:00 a.m. I saw and heard nothing during that time.

As day broke the morning of the 29th, we got a fire mission. German troops were coming through the pass below us. We fired upon the bridge crossing the stream and destroyed it. We were told later that

"What do you think, are they going to kill us?"
I said "It looks that way."

this mountain pass was where Hannibal and his elephants crossed the Alps.

A battalion of German soldiers had invaded our position and had moved into the other forts and the surrounding land. Unfortunately, our command had put us in the center fort. As the firing became more intense, our headquarters in Briançon, which was below us, said to hold the enemy off until they could evacuate. We were then to begin to retreat.

During that time, Dale Blank, Ralph Beil, Howard Seibels and I had been at an outside wall firing at the advancing krauts. We had destroyed three machine gun squads, killed two more as they attempted to set up, and caused many more killed or wounded as they moved in to surround us. We all ran out of ammo. Things were quite confusing as everyone was trying to decide the best way to retreat from the fort. The Germans now had all our escape routes covered by machine gun fire. Two of our officers had been killed. I heard the men say that one of the officers had run to a lower outside wall, said "follow me" and went over and was gone. A German machine gun later covered that escape route. Apparently a lot of our men left early because only about 40 of the Company remained to be captured.

After it was determined that chances of escape had eluded us, we all gathered in a central passage to await our fate. While we all made our guns inoperable, one of the men donated his white underwear to be used as white flags. A flag was posted at each end of the tunnel until the German in charge ordered us out.

We were very fortunate that this German officer was a good soldier. Other Germans wanted to kill us all, and others wanted to kill those of us who spoke German or French, as traitors or spies. Finally, they set up two machine guns on the wall behind us. They were manned by young soldiers who appeared to be fifteen or sixteen years old. They were shaking so bad, the guns were moving. Then they ordered us to line up against a wall behind us. The guy beside me asked "What do you think, are they going to kill us?" I said "It looks that way."

But instead of giving the order to start shooting, they had us, one by one, step forward to be searched. What a relief that was! Only then could we relax a little and stop shaking and sweating. I don't know of anyone wetting his pants, but it was hard to hold back.

Then they marched us through their rear area and down the mountain to the pass where we had destroyed the bridge. The German engineer, a Major, was furious when he saw us, wanted to kill us, but settled for us carrying a lot of logs to the bridge site. We had killed several of his men. Eventually, we ended up in Italy after several days of confinement and traveling. We had just left Italy two weeks before.

A strange thing happened along the way to a prison in Torino. We were joined by five American prisoners, captured in Southern France also. They were a Marine Major, three Marine Sergeants, and one Frenchman in the fourth Marine Sergeant's uniform who had been killed. They had parachuted into France five days before we invaded. Theirs had been a special mission, which they would not discuss with us.

Corporal Floyd Grissom was hit...we bandaged him and he was able to continue.

One more highlight to this story. There was one non-83rd man captured with us at the fort. His name was Paul Bailey. He was with the 180th Regiment, 45th Division. His squad was left to support us with their 57mm anti-tank gun. In the confusion, he ended up with us. I learned later at the POW camp, that he lived only 30 miles from me in Pennsylvania.

William C. Ford:

On August 27th, "A" and "C" Companies of the 83rd were made part of a provisional task force protecting the right flank of the U.S. 7th Army from Ste. Paul to Albertsville. Our thinly-manned front covered a distance of over 135 miles. Our immediate assignment was to establish a defensive position east of the city of Briançon in Fort Dauphine near the border of Italy.

We moved into position under cover of darkness and set up our mortars. After I had set my mortar up, Captain Smith ordered me to go to an outpost. This outpost was between two and three winding road miles out in front of our lines of defense. My order was to observe a bridge that our forces had blown up to prevent the enemy from crossing the mountains from Italy with tanks and other equipment. In case the enemy started rebuilding the bridge, I was to call back for mortar fire on it. Our mortar platoon had the bridge zeroed-in. I left Corporal Kaufemen in charge of my squad.

I was given one man from each squad. I took Corporal Floyd Grissom, Pfc. Alfred Sheats, and Pfc. Melvin Beaty with me to the outpost. We also had a a radio operator to take with us.

We relieved some men from the 45th Infantry Division who had originally blown the bridge. They cautioned us to be careful about our movements and to stay concealed and low at all times. We had to be especially cautious because our thin front lines that extended about 135 miles wide, had large gaps which gave the enemy every advantage to infiltrate.

The pillbox we occupied was about 500 yards up the mountain from the road that led to the blown bridge, and we had a clear view of that site. All during the day we watched for enemy activity through binoculars, but we saw none. It was very tense being so far in front of our own lines with so few men and very little ammunition.

We could not see the bridge once darkness fell, so we listened to hear if we could detect any activity out there. Around midnight, we could hear the sound of vehicles moving in the vicinity of the bridge. I called Captain Smith and told him there was noise coming from the bridge. He told me to take a patrol out and learn what was really going on. I only had four men beside myself, so I asked for one volunteer to go with me. Pfc. Sheats volunteered, and we set out for the bridge.

Soon we were close enough to the bridge that we could not only hear but we could also see men working on the bridge. We saw a few trucks and other equipment with them. I got back to the pillbox, called Captain Smith, who ordered our mortars to fire. We could see our shells exploding on the bridge, and soon it was destroyed again. Two German Mark IV tanks had already crossed the bridge before we destroyed it. I called back and reported the tanks to Captain Smith. The tanks were forced to stay on the road, because it was narrow with high banks on either side. Captain Smith put down mortar fire and destroyed both tanks before they got rolling good.

In a short time the Germans began firing mortars and artillery barrages all along our mountainside. I ordered my men to get out of

Sometimes the enemy would come very close to us.
We could hear them talking.

the pillbox and take up a position about fifty yards up the mountain.
We were soon under infantry attack. I called back to Captain Smith
and told him about the German infantry firing on us. He told me to
hold on to our position, so we began to return rifle fire to the
Germans. We learned by radio that our forces on the main defensive
line were under heavy attack, and that "C" Company was surrounded
by the infiltrated Germans. We also got a report that the enemy had
advanced on Fort de Trois Têtes positions and were boxing our
"C" Company men at Briançon.

The enemy continued rifle and burp gun fire toward us. We returned
fire, but soon ran out of ammunition. I called Captain Smith, told him
this, and he ordered me to pull back to our lines. I had to make a
decision which way to move, because the shells were bursting all
around, and hitting big trees, spraying us with shrapnel and wood
splinters. I decided to lead my men up the mountain instead of
toward the road. I told the radio operator to destroy the radio so the
enemy couldn't use it.

We moved up a ditch under burp gun and rifle fire. Only one man,
Corporal Floyd Grissom, was hit. Fortunately none of his bones were

broken, so we bandaged him and he was able to continue. The fir trees had low branches, which gave us some cover from the enemy.

We thought about surrendering to the enemy, but we all agreed not to, and to continue trying to get out of this trap. I always had a horror about becoming a prisoner of war. I also had a fear of being picked off by a sniper and killed in the mountains with no one knowing where I was and left for the dogs or some other wild animals to eat me. This had always bothered me, and I did not want this to happen. Though if it did, I would not know it.

Sometimes the enemy would come very close to us. We could hear them talking. We continued to work our way up the mountain, doing more crawling than anything else. Once we got to the top, we ran into a Frenchman who identified himself as a FFI man, and showed us his FFI card. We were not sure at first who we had made contact with. We could only speak a few words of French, and he could speak no English. We tried to explain to him that we were cut off from our main forces and were trying to get back to our lines. He seemed to understand, and led us through the rough terrain and rocks. We finally made it to our lines. If we had not made contact with the FFI, I probably would have led my men right into the enemy's hands, because the last order I'd received was to work our way back to Briançon, which our forces had abandoned. All American units had withdrawn and established a new defensive line near Col de Lauderet.

Although out-flanked by the enemy, "C" Company continued to fight the enemy on all sides, inflicting many casualties. When the order had come to pull back to Col de Lauderet, our medics stayed with our wounded men in Briançon.

We continued vigorous combat patrols all that night. We had patrols going in all directions to keep the enemy from advancing up the valley. As our patrols continued to clash with the enemy during the night, they were very successful. The enemy did not advance. The next day, September 1st, we were relieved from the front lines by an Infantry rifle company. We moved to Bourgain to reorganize and re-equip. We needed some new men to replace our heavy losses. We also lost a lot of equipment in the retreat.

Robert B. Smith:

(Excerpts from letters written on September 4th, 19th and 28th by Captain Smith to his wife Annette):

I guess August 29 will always live as one of the blackest days of my life... anyway, my Company distinguished itself and I received a verbal commendation in behalf of the Corps for the Company.

I have lost everything I own except the clothes I have on. The things I had in my pockets, and my field glasses and rifle, are all I have left. We killed many, many Germans both by hand and with our mortars. The men in this Company were wonderful, and I am going to try to get the Congressional Medal of Honor for my Company Executive (First Lieutenant Andre N. Laus). He was a real officer and a brave man, and many of the men were the same calibre. One Sergeant killed four Germans by himself and the other officers were tops, as well as non-coms. Anyway, that's all over and we'll be up and at 'em soon.

Our Company had to stop for a while to train new replacements and to re-equip, since we lost most of our equipment, but have it all back now and are ready to go. We still have the same old "C" Company spirit. There are about 50 krauts hiding in a woods about a mile from here, so yesterday we took a patrol out to try and locate them. I sent one Lieutenant back to get a couple of squads to bring up for a reserve. I told him to ask for volunteers, and I thought he could get up a couple of squads. When I got back to the woods the whole damn Company was there. They had all volunteered, so you can see what "C" Company is like. We never did find the krauts. We did find an ammunition dump and destroyed that.

I remember the night we were going into position in a mountainous section of France, and I could look back and see the balance of the Company following up the narrow, winding road. And it was "C" Company, my company, and I was so proud of them. Well, most of that company is still with me, a hell of a good company; yes, the best in the Battalion.

We re-took the place where we went into position there later, and I did find my prayer book that Preacher Lewis gave me, and the little Bible you put in my bag, some odds and ends of underwear, socks, etc., of mine scattered around. Anyway, that's a story that will have to wait.

I found my Company Exec's grave there, too. He was a brave man and a damn good soldier and officer. I have a new Company Exec now. He is also a damn good soldier and officer. He got nicked in the leg by a machine gun bullet that day, but it just brought the blood barely through the skin, so he didn't mention it for a day or two. Me? I didn't get a scratch and never will now. You know I always had an

While back for a rest, we captured a bunch of prisoners.

obsession that I would depart this world during my 37th year. I guess I dreamed it one time when I was a kid. Well, I was 38 yesterday, so I'm over the hump now. Don't ever worry now. I'll guarantee to make it from here on.

Raymond (Pop) Hoover:

It was a very "hot" spot. Somehow when we evacuated, I lost my wedding ring. Two weeks later when we were able to return, I recognized my old foxhole, saw something shiny, jumped inside, and found my wedding ring!

Andrew C. Leech:

We were relieved for awhile, and moved about six miles back of the lines to a bivouac area. As everyone was unloading, to our surprise, someone stumbled into five Krauts asleep in the woods. One was an officer. He jumped to his feet and pulled his gun, but too late. There was a whole Company coming at them, so they reached for the sky, giving up their guns.

The next day we moved to a new area, leaving our kitchen to come on later. One of the kitchen boys went out into a potato patch and came upon some Jerries lying in the potatoes. He ran back, grabbed a rifle, and hollered "Jerries!" The rest of the boys grabbed their rifles and

ran after him. They came to the edge of the potato patch and saw
one's head peep up. Joe T. Owens cracked down on him and hollered
"Come out of there!" They did, hands shot up all around, and out
walked five more Jerries. One was an officer who said they had come
up from the south and were trying to get back to their lines.

We had quite a few laughs out of moving back to the rear to capture a
bunch of prisoners.

In our rapid advance from the south, the Jerries had been cut off and
fled to the woods. The FFI rounded up many of these after our troops
had gone through. At the next town, civilians there told us that as we
moved in, several Jerries ran out the other side of town. We sent out
several voluntary patrols and searched the woods nearby, and did bag
one more.

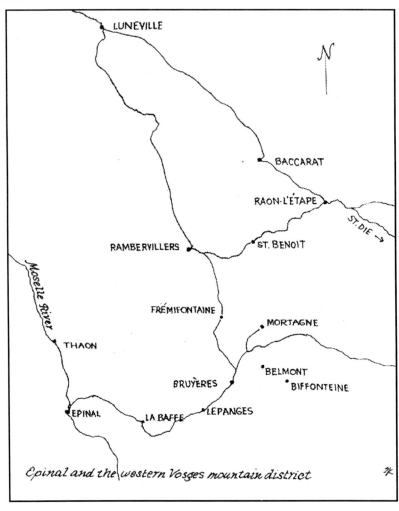

Epinal and the western Vosges mountain district

Into The Vosges Mountains

Abandoning the Rhone Valley and a large part of central France as indefensible, the Germans stiffened their resistance as they withdrew to the Vosges Mountains that form a natural barrier to the Rhineland, just above Switzerland. They had fought the French in this area in the 1870's, and again in the First World War, and knew the ground very well. The Vosges are superbly suited for defense. Never in the long history of European warfare had an attacking army successfully crossed the Vosges. The 83rd was assigned to the Sixth Corps, made up of the 3rd, 36th, and 45th Divisions, and a special unit, the Nisei 442nd Regimental Combat Team. As the Vosges front slowly moved, our 83rd provided fire support at various times to all four.

Audie Murphy, the Congressional Medal of Honor winner from the 3rd Division, who had been in combat since the invasion of Sicily, described the months in the Vosges as having been "some of the toughest fighting of the entire war".

Having been backed up closer to Germany by now, the Jerries were sometimes fanatical. When some French resistance fighters shot a couple of German soldiers in Ste. Die, the entire village was burned to the ground, without a single house being spared. We moved through smoking Ste. Die to the neighboring village of Ste. Marie aux Mines, which had been a French strongpoint in World War I, and saw how powerful the hatred for Germans was among the civilians, whose first language ironically, was German. About a dozen of their women had fraternized with Jerries, and the villagers had shaved their heads completely bald.

Andrew C. Leech:

Epinal, on the Moselle River was a place of bitter fighting. The Germans blew up all the bridges and our Infantry crossed on ropes, waded, or used amphibious DUKWs. Our losses were heavy here. After crossing and taking the town, the Jerry losses were very heavy. So many on both sides were killed here that it was said to be a place where brave men died.

We moved into Epinal and set up in an old college and stayed for about a week. We then moved up to Destord, set up and stayed a few days, and pushed on to Fremifontaine, and one platoon set up in Autry in an old Catholic mission. We had some heavy fighting in these two towns and broke up several counterattacks. Next we moved

*They moved right into our mortar positions
with machine pistols and hand grenades.*

to Luneville supporting the 44th Division which was newly arrived here from the States.

We had some rugged fighting here for a couple of weeks, and it rained almost daily putting us in a sea of water and mud. It snowed a couple of times. One morning we had planned a full scale attack in this sector and woke up to find everything covered with snow.

The attack went on according to plan but bogged down as our doughboys became perfect targets advancing in the snow. Even worse, our tanks and heavy artillery could not get off the roads so our losses were heavy and our gain was very little. However, in a couple of days the snow melted and we jumped off again one morning before daylight into another attack — one in which Kimbrough was killed. We gained several little towns and finally we were relieved from this division and went back to join the 36th Division.

It was here that the Germans mounted a counterattack which flanked a town and came down off a mountainside one morning just after daylight. They moved right into our mortar positions before we knew it and had our second platoon surrounded. They opened up all around us with machine pistols, machine guns, hand grenades and the like. We had one outpost with four men on a machine gun and BAR. Our outpost opened up and mowed down quite a few of the onrushing Jerries before they killed our gunner and finally wiped out our outpost with the exception of two of our boys who got away. They next overran our position and began shooting our boys in their foxholes and throwing hand grenades in with them. They killed several of our men including our lieutenant and the remainder were taken prisoner, except for eight or ten that managed to get away, and I was among that number.

The Germans next advanced across an open field toward the town where our other platoon was set up. The platoon had time to get ready for them and opened up with everything they had. Our men mowed down quite a few, stopping the attack before they could get into town. It was our Company that had broken up the attack of about three companies of Jerries and saved the town because the Infantry had been surrounded and cut off.

Lee Steedle:

We had a tragedy in our platoon, involving a Frenchwoman and an officer we should not have lost. Although we enlisted men were not permitted to marry even pregnant civilian women, John M. Taylor, one of our platoon officers had somehow managed to marry a Frenchwoman some months earlier, and she received his support allotment. When he learned for certain that she was profligately unfaithful, he was badly affected. We all knew that Taylor was depressed. He was a brave officer, but a real character. He constantly wore a fur-lined black Air Corps jacket, even when he was up at an OP where he could more easily be spotted by the Jerries.

One day, returning down the mountain from the OP with Marion Bailey, they came to a fork in the trail. Bailey said "Hey, Lieutenant Taylor — you're taking the wrong fork!" Lieutenant Taylor replied: "Are you sure you know the way? Then see you later!" and disappeared along the wrong trail, while a very worried Bailey returned to the platoon and told us about it. We never saw John Taylor alive again. The following day, a farmer came to us and said he had picked up and moved to his barn, the body of a shot American officer. Ours.

I picked up another part of this story a few years later when reading Audie Murphy's account of the time we had been supporting his 3rd

Division. In his book, *To Hell and Back*, Murphy told of calling for fire from our chemical mortars. Three pages later, while still in the same position, he wrote of warning an officer wearing an Air Corps jacket who had walked up to his outpost, not to go further. Murphy told him there were only Jerries ahead. The officer ignored his advice, and continued on. Murphy said that the following morning, following an attack, they came upon the officer's body. Murphy's comment was: "His kind never learns!" My feeling is that John Taylor had learned, too much, but that he just couldn't handle it.

Fred G. Rand:

When Lieutenant Taylor was killed, I was transferred from "A" Company to "D" Company's platoon that had Wofford Jackson as Platoon Sergeant. The night I was taken to "D", I met Jackson for the first time. He gave me a jeep driver and a radio operator, and I went and reported directly to the C.O. of the 100th Battalion, 442nd Regimental Combat Team.

I directed our mortar fire in support of these Nisei troops when they were fighting to relieve the "Lost Battalion" of the 36th Division's 141st Infantry, which had been surrounded for seven days at Biffontaine, near Bruyeres. Since Jerry held the road approach, the only way to relieve the battalion was to take a steep ridge high above the fighting. Three times the 442nd attacked the ridge, and three times they were thrown back with heavy losses. When they assaulted

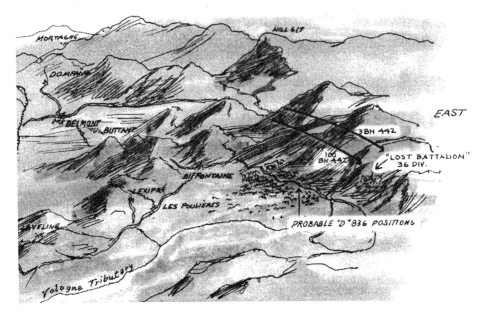

Nisei 442nd Combat Team rescues the "Lost Battalion".

the ridge for the fourth time, it had been so heavily mortared that it looked as though it had been swept by a forest fire.

The 442nd did succeed, and the Lost Battalion was relieved, but in that battle the 442nd suffered tremendous casualties. Nearly 2,000 of their men — a number representing almost half of their unit strength — were hospitalized as a result of that action, and 140 had been killed. The loss was so severe that the Nisei, no longer operational, were sent back down to Marseilles to reorganize with new Japanese-American replacements. By war's end, that most-decorated of all American units, whose organizational strength — totally volunteer — normally totaled 4,200, had suffered 9,486 casualties, with 600 fatalities. Nowhere else have I ever seen the high degree of selflessness and commitment they gave. America's abuse of their families during this war is a disgrace for which I hope they can some day forgive us.

Sam Kweskin:

JUST ANOTHER DAY. For some reason, our jeep — Colin Klatt driving — was held up, and I hoisted myself from the back seat and asked Paul Troia to pull my sketch-book from the musette bag on my back.

It was chilly, my fingers were numb despite GI-issue woolen gloves. I withdrew a black grease pencil from a pocket and clambered off the road, along the berm.

What I saw within the tall fir and pine forest were Infantry of the 36th (Texas) Division, huddling along the roadside, warming their hands over a Sterno can or a small fire of twigs and scrap.

Hoping the jeep wouldn't move for awhile, I sketched what I saw as I looked into their faces. They were unshaven, with a gaunt, weary look in their eyes. I could feel and see in their eyes all the misery and sadness and hopelessness of man's misplaced efforts to live in peace. Perhaps that 33-year-old husband looking up at me was actually only 21. Was it possible, I thought, the bags under those eyes have bags of their own?

The men in these holes around me hadn't started the war, but it was they who might have to die for a cause. I finished the sketch just as our jeep gunned forward.

As we came to our destination a few hundred feet from the men I had drawn, I saw that here, in a forest near Biffontaine, there was a clearing to our right. It was little more than a rectangle paralleling the road, sunken below the shoulder, and maybe only 150 feet long and 50 feet wide. At the far end of this field, a hill rose with its myriad pine-tops lost in the haze that surrounded us this high up.

I saw a squad of GI's and a couple of 4.2's in position, and guessed this was part of the platoon we were relieving.

Strangely, standing in the middle of this miniature football field, stood a stark white German army ambulance, its rear door open, with bedsheets flowing from it.

Coming closer, we heard a "zipppp!" of artillery — incoming — and tree bursts began to explode ahead of us. Set too high, the shrapnel dropped harmlessly before us, but we didn't wait to admire the fireworks. The squads in the small meadow were already scurrying into dugouts, and we jumped from our jeeps to find shelter — any kind!

In retrospect, I didn't do a wise thing by running across the field at an angle, but I was aiming for a huge stump of a tree that sat before a farm house at the far end — "the goal-post end" — of the field.

I hooked the stump with my left arm and swung into an arc to place myself behind it, away from the explosions, now hitting with stomach-churning rapidity onto and above the small meadow.

Immediately, another man in our squad was grabbing my left elbow, and repeated the slide, this time to land on his stomach behind me.

There came the nerve-wracking moment of wanting to do something like dig my fingernails into the bark, and deposit myself into the middle of the trunk!

There was silence. When we arose we saw that two of the Infantry's 81mm crew, that had also been there when we arrived, were wounded. It made me wonder — as in Italy — if I had come to a "hot zone" that I had been told was "a snap".

Now we did what we had come for. Within an hour we had taken over the guns, aligned their coordinates, and begun firing in support of the 442nd Combat Team — Nisei soldiers — later to become the most decorated unit in the war. This was to become one of their most courageous and valorous moments — the Nisei were fighting to free a surrounded battalion of the 36th Division in this action, supported by fire from our "D" Company mortars.

Our rounds left their tubes at about forty a minute, and the vale reeked of cordite, cosmolene and smoke.

Our squad had positioned itself practically in the center of the small meadow, where between us and the road was a patch of corn stalks, no more than twenty by ten feet in area. For some unaccountable reason, the ambulance still stood — and would for another day — like a white flag to notify the Germans that maybe there were Americans hanging around it!

We fired almost continually at the German positions, all four guns of the platoon barking like all the dogs of war gone mad.

Each round carried more fire power than a 105 mm artillery shell and we fired many more rounds per minute than an artillery howitzer could.

I had taken over a dugout, three feet deep, about seven feet long, and three feet wide, with logs and sandbags over it. I shared the tight fit with Paul Troia, a native of New York City.

We were shelled again the following day, and Sergeant Yacubisin had been close to my dugout under the trees when the Minnenwerfer — "Screaming Meemees" — started coming in. He quickly scrambled into my dugout, lying atop me, until the barrage lifted. "Yak" reached out for his helmet that had fallen at the entrance to the dugout just as a heavy branch snapped under an exploding shell and fell directly upon the helmet at the tip of his fingers, narrowly missing crushing his hand. And now another GI from the close-by 36th Division 81mm mortar platoon was wounded by the same barrage.

Night. It began to drizzle and slowly trickled under the raincoat that I'd placed close to the entrance. It began to get uncomfortable in my sandbagged hole, and I pushed myself feet first out of it. I grabbed a blanket, and carefully made my way through the darkness to the darkened farmhouse. At least it was warm in there, and a few of the GIs had decided to bunk there. A Coleman lantern lit up one of the rooms, and I turned to the small room the farmer was seated in. Strange, he hadn't left his farm, even through all the shelling. He had probably been here throughout the German occupation, and would be here until he died, peacefully, in old age.

I sat myself to his side; he looked up once, and went back to reading a book, his head resting on one hand, a candle flickering nearby. But I had come in for a definite purpose: here was the stove, and here was where I could dry my blankets.

I was due to relieve one of the crew at the gun position, where we had been laying down harassing fire to keep the Germans awake... and nervous. I opened the blankets to dry in the confined room, and went into the darkness.

Standing at the doorway for a moment, hearing only the clink of metal or a muffled voice from our gun position, I endeavored to adjust my eyesight to the blackness around me. By feel and sound I slowly made my way to our position, a little behind the central portion of the corn patch.

By the mutter of voices, I knew I was coming closer, and was finally able to orient myself a bit more by feeling the cornstalks. Using them as a guide with my left hand, I edged along the outer stalks and walked to where I remembered there was a small footpath through the corn to where our mortar stood.

There seemed to be some difficulty that the fellows on the other side were encountering, but I couldn't make out what it was.

As I was about to make a sharp left into the footpath, *something* told me to continue instead, all the way around the square of stalks, and thereby take a little longer to get to the gun.

Just as I took the first step away from the path, the gun fired,

"...the gun sent the shell whizzing low, behind my head"

sending the shell whizzing, low, behind my head and into the sky! I broke into a cold sweat, wetter than the drizzle about us.

Finally able to get around to the gun, I learned that the crew had dismounted the barrel because a shell had stuck in it. And as they lowered the barrel from the unipod, the shell had gained heat, slid down the melting cosmoline, hit the firing pin and fired, propelling the 25-pound 4.2 shell out of the barrel.

Since the barrel had been lowered at the time, the shell streaked out at about the height of my head as I had momentarily paused in the footpath. Within that split second, I had decided to walk away from the path, and that — and a God watching over me — saved my life.

I began to tremble uncontrollably, and rationalized to my buddies that it was only the cold and the rain. Finally, we realized the gun had some inoperative defect, and we shut it down.
JUST ANOTHER DAY!

Fred G. Rand, Jr.:
When "D" Company went into Sainte Marie aux Mines on November 24th, we had not had a bath for a long time in the cold Vosges Mountains. Even though the Germans had stripped these people of their food and fuel, they were so pleased that we had saved their town, that the townspeople gave of their remaining fuel to fire up the boilers in the public bathhouse, and invited us to bathe as their guests. We lined up with clean clothes, soap and towels and listened to the ones in front say "Ahhhhhh!"

It was much too long a time later that we had another opportunity to get clean. A QM shower unit was set up at a farm. Members of our platoon were loaded on a truck, and we went to the location of the shower truck. Then Julius Sorrenson and I got into a jeep and followed a short time later, along one of those tree-lined roads. All of a sudden, the first German plane we had seen in a long time came strafing toward us. We rolled out of the jeep, down the shoulder of the road. Then we realized the plane was headed toward the shower, still strafing. When we got there we saw a very unhappy person. After he had showered and put on clean clothes, the plane came over. He had dived under a fence beside the road where the shower truck sat. What he dove into was a very wet, muddy pig pen, and he was covered with muck. Yes, they gave him another turn at the shower.

Cleanliness and good eating were rare in combat, but in one little village we saw a goose walking down the road, and thought about how good it might taste. Two of us traded our rations for the goose,

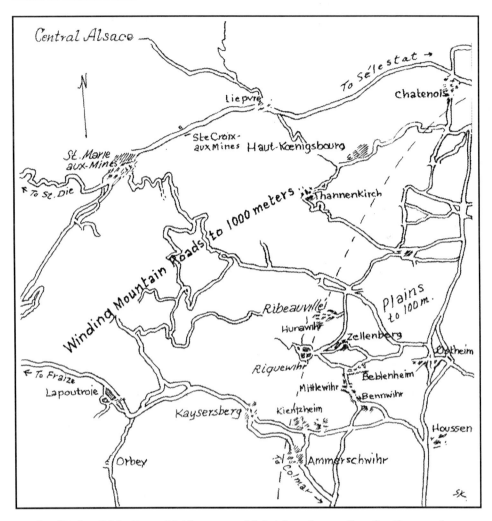

and a little old lady said if we would let her have the feathers, she would kill it and pick the feathers off. Another woman let us cook the goose in her oven. While the goose was cooking, I opened some canned vegetables from our 10-in-1 rations, and set them on the stove. A little while later, I noticed the can of corn had been moved to the drainboard. I put the can back on the stove. Still later it was back on the drainboard. Shaking her head, the woman said "Non manges!", people don't eat corn, that's only for hogs or chickens.

Well we did have a good goose dinner, while a horrified woman shuddered watching us eat "hog food".

One of the best things about our 10-in-1 rations was the canned bacon. There was always a lot of wonderful grease to go with potatoes, etc. But it took this Texas boy to know its full potential.

When I saw how much bacon grease was left over, I asked the cooks to send up some flour. The next night when I came back from the OP, there was the flour, and I said I'd make gravy. I was told I couldn't make gravy without chicken, ham, turkey, etc. I said stick around. I borrowed a large skillet, put in some bacon grease, and a lot of flour and browned them over the heat while pouring in milk and stirring. Fortunately I had made a lot of it. With some crackers from the rations and some of locals' dark, heavy bread, this skilletful went quickly.

The kitchen people who sent up the rations could not understand why all the flour was being ordered in the next few days. Each night when I came in from the OP, bacon grease gravy was being, or had been, prepared. They'd learned from this Texas boy raised in the country, how good bacon grease gravy could be. Too bad we didn't have some grits to go with it!

Sam Kweskin:

JUST WHEN I THOUGHT I'D HAVE A FULL NIGHT'S SLEEP:
About twenty miles north of Ste. Die, is a village much like any other in the Vosges Mountains. Moussey, miles from any main road, complete with canal, the central town pump, laughing children. I remember a girl of about twelve, running from her mother and sweeping her arms around my shoulders while planting a large kiss on my cheek. "Merci!" she cried as she ran back, red-faced to her mother "Merci a nos liberateurs!"

And so it was here, after I'd been transferred to HQ Company, that two HQ officers went one drizzly afternoon to check on the security and appropriateness of a chateau at the edge of the village. Captain Ed Trey and Major John McEvoy found it deserted, but did an obligatory search of the premises, not overlooking the coal bin. They returned to our base, giving the go-ahead to move HQ Company forward into Moussey and thereby keep close to the weapons companies.

We hadn't seen an edifice such as this since "Citizen Kane", and all of us jumped at the chance to sleep in real beds.

The library, I remember, had numerous books, many of them early — if not first — editions in French, English, and German. One of the titles I remembered as being "Robinson Crusoe" in a morocco binding. The building's exterior had two turreted towers at the front corners, and a large porch between them, with staircases going up at either end. It was about four or five stories high and must have incorporated twenty rooms. A driveway from the village ran through a private park for about two blocks before one came upon this Laederich Mansion.

I was troubled as to why an educated man, such as Monsieur Laederich, was not around to care for the treasures of books, porcelain, statuary, and Meissen. Could he have been a collaborator? Then why not remove the expensive items, and flee with them to Germany? Was he a patriot? If so, and he was jailed, or worse, why had the Germans not requisitioned the fine art in this marvelous domicile? It was a question I would never have answered.

But to show that we, upstanding Americans that we were, could also respect personal belongings — it was a certainty that high-ranking Germans must have occupied this building — we were warned by one of our officers not to "liberate" ANY item of the Laederich family. It seemed that no single book was missing, so the Germans must have respected the owner's acquisitions.

All settled in, we chowed down, bringing food from the kitchen which was in the basement, protected by renaissance window bars protecting us from any inroads, human or otherwise.

Came the evening, I ascended a winding concrete staircase to one of the many guest rooms, finding one with a large bed and dark mahogany dresser, and a closet containing dinner clothes — and of all things — a top hat.

I believe T/5 Dave Chapman and I shared the big bed. Candlelight permitted us to find our way around the building, but winter weather and nightfall militated against wandering around too much, and we hit the sack.

About 5:00 in the morning a huge explosion roared through the building. I was tossed out of my side of the bed. Wearing only shorts and sweatshirts Chapman and I threw our feet into loose boots, grabbed our carbines, and ran out the door. Doug Swayze and Jake Miringoff ran by, both having been knocked out of bed. The whole center of the Chateau was demolished — Captain Robert Edwards said when he looked out the door on the second floor, he could see all the way to the basement.

Below us, the entire stone staircase had been destroyed, leaving just jagged pieces of stone. Here and there spears of the oaken banister thrust themselves into the air, and choking concrete dust pervaded the entire area.

Other GIs below were rushing about to find the source of the explosion, and Chapman and I somehow made our way over the broken concrete slabs to the floor below.

We ran out into the cold, and saw Sergeant Kermit Jorgensen throwing a blanket over the trembling body of Paul Cuva, who had a head and hand injury.

Cuva had just been coming off guard duty when he'd walked into the kitchen for hot coffee. Sergeant George Borkuis offered him a cup just as a time bomb — where else, but hidden in the coal pile behind the kitchen wall — exploded, rending half the kitchen, and sending huge pots and shards of metal kitchen ware flashing through the room. Amazingly, there were no fatalities, although several men were wounded.

Quickly, the hierarchy decided this wasn't a place to remain. Dog-robbers now went about packing their officers' equipment, while the rest of us somehow got our clothes on, packed our gear, and threw ourselves into our jeeps.

A time bomb exploded...sending huge pots and shards of metal kitchen ware flashing through the room.

Oh, and one more thing.

The officer who had pointed out the morality of leaving everything as we had found it, ordered his enlisted aide to rope together at least twenty of those books of Monsieur Laederich's and — once secured — had them placed gently into his jeep.

Lee Steedle:

Probably my closest call of the entire war had a happy ending because of rations.

We were occupying a position at the edge of dense woods, with our mortars facing a wide field covered with deep snow. A narrow strip of forest jutted out about thirty yards into the field, and we had set up a well-concealed machine gun at the tip of that point. We had dug a deep, standing foxhole behind the gun, and had strung wire to it for a field telephone.

It was late afternoon when my turn came to rotate at that gun. Jerry must have seen movement, and was walking some 88mm fire along the edge of the field, but still more than a hundred yards from me,

Grateful for whoever caused me to hunker down real deep for that phone call.

so I wasn't much concerned. Then the phone rang, with one of the men in my squad telling me that short rations had come up for that evening and the following day, and asking how they should be divided.

The noise ahead of me was getting louder, and not being able to make out exactly what he was saying, I stuck a finger in my other ear and crouched all the way down into that deep, narrow hole. Suddenly I was slammed by concussion, and the machine gun and a couple of sandbags went flying away. Stunned, I slowly cleared my ringing head and got out from under the rocks and dirt that had toppled onto me. An 88 had landed directly in front of me, making a black scorch streak straight across the top of the hole, where it had blown away all the snow and the machine gun. I've always been grateful for whoever it was who shorted our rations and caused me to hunker down real deep for that phone call.

Sam Kweskin:
THAT WASN'T A RIBBON I FELT AROUND MY NECK:
Well, this is not a story about heroism, or courage, or valor. It's a story that — for one frightening moment — had me facing at least twenty years in a stockade, if not hanging at the end of a noose. (You interested yet? You don't HAVE to read this. I just want to get it off my chest).

We were somewhere in the Vosges. Come evening, here with a platoon of "D" Company, Staff/Sergeant Wofford Jackson volunteered me for perimeter guard that night.

It was the usual "two and four": two hours on, to be replaced by another GI for two hours, and be awakened by the third man going off his two-hour tour. I was on my first shift, from eight to ten p.m.

I sat huddled in an overcoat enveloping an M43 field jacket, itself over an OD sweater, shirt, and undershirt. I wore heavy twill trousers *over* my OD pants, both tucked into shoe-pacs under which were two pairs of woolen socks. Would you guess from this description of my habiliments that it was cold? I don't think I ever experienced the cold more anywhere — even in my home-town Chicago in December — than I did in the Vosges Mountains that night.

Before me, as I sat hunched, looking into total darkness, was a .50 calibre machine gun, which I prayed had not frozen. My helmet sat over a wool stocking cap which allowed only my eyes an open space. The well-meaning Canton, Ohio American Legion Ladies Auxiliary didn't know that wearing this gift would inhibit one's hearing.

Within five minutes I had removed the head covering, so that I could better serve that platoon of great guys behind me who were counting on my nerves of steel and eagle eyes (as well as hound's ears) to protect them against the evil forces of Nazi Germany. As a matter of fact — now that fifty-odd years have passed behind us — I've worked up the candor to say that being awarded at least the Congressional Medal of Honor just for being out there did pass before my mind's eyes.

After a while, the lobes of my ears lost any feeling they may have had. I knew they were still part of my anatomy only when I flicked at them with my fingers, at which point they sounded like old leather cracking. My fingers weren't in much better shape, and I knew I still owned toes because when I shook them they felt like unfelt items hitting the sides of my shoes.

Having endured this for two hours, I crawled to the dugout of my relief and awakened him. He in turn, slid from the dugout to the gun, as his eyes adjusted to the terrain. I silently hunched back to my own hole, attempting not to wake Paul Troia, and within seconds I was fast asleep.

There seemed to be some noise that woke me, and on opening my eyes I saw it was daylight! "Wait!!" I said to myself, "Shouldn't I have pulled one more tour between two and four a.m.? The sun shone through the firs and evergreens, and I looked at my PX Elgin. "CRIPES!" I yelled to no one in particular, "It's almost eight a.m.!"

Squads were preparing a firing mission, and the realization was hitting me, hard, that I had missed my middle of the night shift! I looked around, suddenly hoping no one saw any of the 6' 4" of me, but fear rose in my throat like an oyster on a string. No medals for me, I thought. More likely a noose!

Suddenly I saw the man I was to have relieved. I grabbed him by the elbow as he was chomping on a concentrated chocolate bar. "WHY DIDN'T YOU WAIT TILL YOU SAW ME GET OUT OF MY DUGOUT? WHY DID YOU LET ME SLEEP THROUGH MY SHIFT? THEY'RE GOING TO HAVE MY NECK, IF NOT OTHER PARTS OF ME!! I GOT A COURT MARTIAL FOR SURE, COMING UP!"

"Sam," he laughed, unfazed by my fright and misery, "I gotta tell you. After I finished the twelve to two stint I couldn't move! I couldn't get myself out of that hole! So I stayed there for four hours more, till six this morning. I tell you, I was so froze, I'd have broken every bone in my body if I had moved! Jackson took me off the outpost at six. Had breakfast, yet?"

"Sam," he laughed, unfazed by my fright and misery, "I gotta tell you..."

Killed By Our Own Defective Shells

The Autumn months of 1944 were the most difficult for the 83rd psychologically, because the entire batch of mortar ammunition we were receiving was suspect. This was not due to the shells themselves, but to their fuses. Something had been changed in the way they were manufactured, and instead of causing the shell to explode upon impact, the fuse would sometimes cause the shell to explode in the barrel, or after a partial rotation in the air, about ten feet after leaving the barrel. Four times in our Battalion, we had these premature bursts which killed or wounded our men. Leonard Blystone of "D" Company was among those killed. He had earned a Bronze Star for bravery, and it is ironic that while the Germans didn't succeed in killing him, a Stateside manufacturer of defective fuses did.

Major General Alden H. Waitt, Chief of Chemical Warfare Services, testified before a Senate Committee in Washington that defective 4.2 shells killed American soldiers during the Fall of 1944. Waitt was a witness in the hearing on war profits of the Midwest munitions manufacturer who produced our fuses.

Reno Toniolo:

I'm sure most of us knew that our shells were being sabotaged in the U.S.A. At Bischweiler we had a shell blow up in the barrel. When I went to pick up Cooper's leg to put a tourniquet on it, it was blown clean off. He survived. Rushing was killed and about four others were wounded by this explosion.

James G. Helsel:

I am reminded of this sad event almost daily. We were staying in a house with a family named Schnell. They had a three year old grandson named Eddie, who took to me like a duck to water. I played with him, gave him candy. Poppa Schnell said I was like a father to Eddie. But we couldn't keep Eddie away from the gun position when we started firing.

The day our Number One gun blew up from a defective shell, killing Corporal Rushing and taking Cooper's leg it also wounded a few others of us. When I got back from the field hospital, A.J. Brown told me Eddie had caught a piece in his heart. When he went to give him First Aid, he saw that Eddie was dead.

Poppa Schnell thanked me and thanked me for having been so good to Eddie. The old man gave me a large hand-carved meerschaum pipe

When he went to give him First Aid, he saw that Eddie was dead.

which I still have. He told me to write to him, which I never did because I can't write in German, and Poppa Schnell didn't speak English. I have a three year old grandson who looks like Eddie, and takes to me the same way, so I am reminded of Eddie often.

Reno Toniolo:

We came upon an Italian living in France who offered to give us welcome relief from GI rations. We had our four mortars set up in a woods near Bischweiler, when along came this Italian civilian asking if anyone spoke his language. Of course, they sent him to me. He told me they were going to butcher that day, and would we like any meat. I went around the platoon and took orders for whatever the guys wanted. He came back later that afternoon with his wife and with piles of juicy red meat.

They stayed around talking to us, while our guys got ready for a feast. Then the Germans began firing ladder fire, trying to seek us out. We all stayed close to our foxholes, because we knew we were going to get it. Still, the couple stayed around. The shells came closer and closer till they started hitting right in our position. There was a large foxhole toward the end of the area. When they came this close, the Italian's wife jumped into the hole first, and then almost a whole squad on top of her.

Hawkins and O'Riley were frying their steaks on a Coleman burner, sitting on their helmets. A shell hit nearby, killing both of them. This was the same place where a shell blew up in one of our mortars, and a little boy was killed by a piece of the shrapnel in his heart.

The shells came closer and closer till they started hitting right in our position.

Stories They Wouldn't Tell On Themselves

First Lieutenant James Lauro, who had been a Company "D" platoon sergeant in Italy, and deservedly received a battlefield commission, composed and sent this poem to a girl back home:

Be not bitter my beloved

Though I've gone from thee,

For the currents we drift on

In this restless sea

Flowed together one brief moment

Moving side by side

Mingled, then diverged forever

On the wayward tide.

Rather, thank those unknown causes

Whose compelling force

Brought the blending of these waters

On their wayward course.

Let that interlude of sunlight

Mid dark passage be

Consummated in the essence of its memory.

Staff / Sergeant Clark Riddle, who later took over the same platoon of Company "D", was still a squad leader when, firing at short range below some terraces in the rain, an unnoticed wet powder bundle was slipped onto a shell fired from his mortar. The shell barely burped out of his barrel, traveled only a few yards, and fortunately landed flat, in the soft mud of the terrace just above his gun. Clark climbed over the wall, saw that the shell's fuse had popped out, meaning that it was fully armed. Gingerly, Clark picked up the shell, and hugging it tightly to himself as if it were a baby, he carefully climbed up over several additional terraces and laid the shell flat. The entire platoon began breathing again, and yelled our congratulations.

Mark Freedom **PAID**

The Colmar Pocket

The fighting in the Vosges Mountains ended with the German withdrawal at the end of November. We GIs didn't know it at the time, and probably wouldn't have cared, but this was the first time in all of European history that an army had punched through the Vosges.

Now we left the mountains, engaging the Germans on the low rolling hills of the wine country, just west of the Rhine. It was here that Jerry fought bitterly to hold one of their last pockets of strength in France — the area surrounding the city of Colmar.

Frederick W. Endlein:

I remember what happened in the Colmar area. We were attached to the 36th Infantry Division. At this time each 83rd company had only two platoons. I was in charge of the ammo detail. Both of our platoons were spread over a ridge to stop the Germans from getting through. The 36th was spread out pretty thin, and the Germans broke through our lines, and in doing so, overran our two platoons. One of our men who escaped, said he saw a German throw a grenade in one of our foxholes, killing everyone inside.

Things got so bad that they gave me orders to set the ammo truck on fire if we had to pull out and leave it. It never came to that, as we finally repelled the attack. Two men in our platoon were killed.

Sam Kweskin:

Having now been assigned to Headquarters Company, I was prepared for anything from KP to guard duty to assisting Lieutenant Bob Brimm publish *Muzzleblasts*.

Often too, I would ride shotgun for whichever officer had to visit front-line companies. This day, Walter Hauser, a prematurely graying First Lieutenant, was assigned to learn what munitions and food, and wearing apparel were needed by two companies on line, each in separate villages.

"Kweskin? You know any volunteers?" he smiled. Well, I looked around and there was no one else in the little bedroom of a house we had taken over.

So I grabbed a carbine, and followed him out the door. Not only was I duty-bound to serve whims and commands of officers, but for personal reasons I found myself putting in more time on the line this way than if I had been in an alphabet company, with a few days at a

*Had we gone on to "B" Company instead of "A",
we might have been among the eleven killed or captured.*

time for R&R.

Jerry DiLucchio was our driver, and Hauser was getting a bonus anyway, because I often served as a French and German interpreter.

Although my diary reads Zellenberg, I really believe we headed for Kaysersberg, the home town of philosopher/humanitarian/doctor Albert Schweitzer.

Before we got there, Hauser stopped at a small crossroads and asked: "Where'll we go first? Over to "B" in Riquewihr, or to "A"? He looked first at Jerry, then turned to me. Not having learned not to volunteer, I said "Let's go to "A", Lieutenant. I have a lot of friends there".

So off we went. I was surprised at my clout. But, what the hell. It was cold, and there was snow on the ground, and maybe we'd find a place to warm our hands in Kayserberg.

Mortar squads were set up along the cobblestone streets twisting through the ancient town. Here and there, a tank was parked. One occasionally stuck its 105mm cannon between a couple of buildings and seemed to make the entire village shake when it let loose a round into the valley where the Germans were dug in. Buildings on either side of the street we rode along must have gone back two hundred years; they leaned with age, and were held up with oaken beams between the whitened plaster walls. Low eaves hung almost to the ground from ancient homes and barns, and the smell of manure packed against walls pervaded the cold, damp air.

Mortar rounds whomped out of barrels, flying over the angled roofs to a destination in Bennwihr, or Beblenheim, or Mittelwihr, and sometimes to the vineyards surrounding those ancient villages.

Hauser and I ascended a rickety staircase in a building which sat highest, overlooking the towns and vineyards to the north and east. We came upon what had been bedrooms on the second floor, and walked into the one facing the front lines.

There were four or five soldiers wearing jackets against the cold, the officers recognizable by the webbed belt and .45 Colt on their hips. Radios, wires, and some rations were on the floor and upon a table in the room's center. Standing behind venetian blinds, two of the officers were gazing through field glasses toward a large plain, on which sat our three target villages. In the haze northeast of us could be seen the Black Forest across the Rhine.

Lieutenant Cameron said a quick "Hello!" and before talking at length with Hauser, looked across the landscape through his binoculars. Puffs of smoke from our high explosive and phosphorus rounds could be seen exploding about a mile down the slope, and I could make out German infantry running from the shelling.

In the streets behind us, mortars were joined by tanks, in communication with observers in our room, in the cacophonous blasts from gun muzzles out of our village.

There was a pall of plaster dust to make us choke and cough in our observation post, added to the noise all about us. The walls doubtless had loosened throughout the top floor.

Suddenly, there appeared at the doorway a breathless GI, shouting above the din, asking if we were all crazy, and a couple of officers were visibly perturbed by his lack of military courtesy. He didn't wait for an answer: "Are you nuts?" he yelled, "You know a German shell just took out the back bedroom? Look for yourselves!" It WAS a

German round that had torn down the other bedroom. Once we saw they had gotten our range, we all made a beeline for anything downstairs!

Fortune had smiled on us — and not just that once that day. For had we gone on to "B" Company instead of "A", we might have been among the eleven men of "B" killed or captured in an SS School graduation exercise — attacking an American gun position. "B" had been firing from the outskirts of Riquewihr when the counterattack occurred. Earl Rapp who survived to become a fine outfielder for the St. Louis Browns and the New York Giants was one of the men who escaped. Rapp hid in a drainage culvert for hours as he heard Germans running back and forth above him. Eventually he made his way back, and was brought over to HQ to report on what happened.

By this time, I had returned to HQ, having learned by radio at "A" about the attack on "B". The Germans withdrew with some of our men as prisoners.

A young recruit had reported in to us with a few other replacements the night before, and he and I had an engaging talk about his having

Earl Rapp hid for hours,
as he heard Germans running back and forth above him.

been in the Metropolitan Opera Ballet Corps. He had asked me what combat was going to be like. He was one of the men lost that day — his very first day in combat.

Lee Steedle:

Our "D" Company platoon occupied Zellenberg, a frying-pan shaped village, with a double row of houses at the handle, leading into a tiny square of stone row houses. No civilians were in sight, just a round and ancient fountain plopping water into its greenish pool from four leaden pipes.

The krauts were in the next village, topping a slightly lower hill just a half-mile further ahead, down a road extending through the far side of our square. None of us liked our gun position. The open area was so small that we'd have to check our barrel elevations after every few rounds to make sure we'd clear the rooflines. Hazardous at night. More cobblestones were removed so we could reset quickly, in case our front would shift.

The silence of the square was disturbing. Still not a single civilian, not even after a room-by-room check around the square. Shutters all closed. Sergeant Yacubisin said "We're the liberazations, but where the hell are the civilians we can be heroes to?" What might the krauts have told them?

A single mortar round came in. Short. The next hit a far rooftop. A third and fourth slammed into the square, and from within our house we could hear the shrapnel ricochet from walls and cobbles. Nothing more. Stillness. Only four rounds and they had zeroed us. We thought the Jerries must have known every inch of this country to have worked so accurately by map. Or else, where could they be observing from?

It was hotter for us that night than we'd expected. Our Infantry hadn't patrolled all the way to the village ahead. Jerry was stiffening. You could see it in the muzzle flashes from his mortars. The sky pulsed with light from their artillery further back. Planes flew over around midnight — German, we could tell from the unsynchronous throbbing of their engines. They were working our roads to Colmar with antipersonnel bombs.

Immediately ahead there was a firefight, as the krauts met our combat patrol with a machine gun waiting somewhere in the vineyards below us. We now fired our mortars short, on the slopes below their village just ahead.

This night the American drive stalled. It was now Jerry's move. Before dawn, the krauts opened their counterattack all along the wide perimeter of our front.

By daylight, our situation became clear. The road we'd moved up the day before had now come under small arms fire. No vehicles could make it by day, and even a well marked ambulance had drawn warning fire. Because we were on the left flank, with all the heavy action to the right, at Colmar, our 4.2 mortars were the only heavy weapons supporting our Infantry battalion ahead. During this period, ammunition for the Infantry 81mm mortars was almost nonexistent because of a supply snafu. We were being called upon to provide more supporting fire than ever. Our full 83rd Battalion was expending approximately 4,000 rounds of mortar ammunition daily. This severely strained our nerves, because we all knew we were still working with defective ammunition that could explode in our barrels.

By afternoon, our Lieutenant brought word we'd be badly needed to help maintain the defensive perimeter around our village this second night. A heavy counterattack was expected immediately to our front.

We were lucky to settle for two casualties this day. Our crews would be out on the guns and suddenly kraut mortar shells would drop in right on top of us. Within the tight square of rooftops you couldn't hear the soft fluffing of their tailfins until just before they landed. Then they'd blast and vomit their shrapnel all around the square.

That night we decided. No full crews in the square. Gunners would set the mortars, and from then on the squad leaders would drop the shells down. Everyone else would be inside doorways nearest the guns. We'd dispersed the ammo to other houses as well as we could. The crews would keep just a few rounds ahead of us, adjusting the powder rings and then dashing out to lay the shells on racks next to our guns. We wanted the minimum of men and ammo exposed.

We hadn't slept for two nights, and the third night was worse. Ammo had come up under cover of darkness, and we were firing constantly. The counter-fire came in accurately, and toward morning Clark Riddle, our Platoon Sergeant received a gaping leg wound. The field ambulance already having been warned away by German artillery rounds, our casualties were being evacuated by gutsy jeep drivers. Clark was tied to a jeep hood, and they raced down the totally exposed Zellenberg road, chased by kraut machine gun fire.

A week later we heard the leg had become gangrenous and had to be amputated. Riddle was going to be married. In quiet times later we wondered — would she still have him?

Months later, we all felt relieved to learn Betty would marry him anyway. "It's only a leg!" she said.

Our situation steadily worsened. The Jerries had reinforced the village ahead, and now wanted ours for its relative height and domination of the main supply road. There was no possibility of our pushing them back. We just hoped to hold on. What now became known as the Battle of the Colmar Pocket had developed into one of the European Theatre's major fights. The Germans had short supply lines, and much more artillery than our side had believed possible. Unlike our Infantry, the Germans clearly had no shortage of ammunition.

Accurate incoming mortar fire continued to cost us casualties. How did they know we were out on the square? Sometimes before we'd even send the first shell on its way, the incoming rounds would come softly fluffing and then blasting into our square, which was now littered by loose cobbles, empty ammo tubes, chunks of masonry, tiles from walls and roofs, and blood.

We were needed on our guns. The krauts by now had established their forward line somewhere in the vines just below us. We were now firing with only a half powder ring, barely enough to propel the shell away, and it traveled only about 300 yards. No one slept.

The final evening, the expected heavy counterattack came, as our square lit up and sounded like hell itself in the constant roar of our mortars, and Jerry's answering fire that came blasting into our position. By now, we had taken eight casualties in our platoon.

During a lull that lasted maybe ten minutes, I went inside to heat some coffee and to cool the sweat and fright that covered me. I heard a sound from our squad room that chilled me. I didn't want to look, I wanted not to have to see him, but forced myself to discover the old man of our squad, 34-year-old Pappy, sobbing uncontrollably. I felt my insides churning as I saw him huddled there, his legs drawn up tightly underneath himself, arms hugging his knees, racked with the great sobs he could not control.

It was war's end for Pappy. He had invaded Sicily, made D-Day at Salerno, the Anzio landing, and our airborne glide into Southern France. Here was the oldest man in our platoon, and arguably one of the bravest, a man with two Purple Hearts who at one time or another had steadied all of us. Now Pappy had received his final

"D" Company OP in upper room.

wound, deep inside him, and he couldn't go on. Each man has his own breaking point, and our Pappy had just gone down. Someone walked him to the medics, and we never saw nor heard from Pappy again.

Morning brought our answer. Two Signal Corps radiomen had been tracking kraut radio emissions, and found that the signals came from the house right next to ours. The transmissions had been in short bursts, and it had taken five days and too many casualties to discover why the krauts had responded to every movement in our platoon. The radio operator was an old civilian, about 70, who had concealed himself in a hollow under a first-floor stairway. He could see through a crack he'd made in the stairs, which gave him a view through the open entrance doorway. He'd always known when we were on the mortars.

Thinking of Clark Riddle, Pappy, and all the others who had gone down here, we knew this old man had no idea how lucky he was to be taken safely away from our anger by the Signal Corps men.

Jerry was moving closer, and toward noon we all realized we could soon be overrun. One man saw Red Goler take off his dog tags and toss them into the fountain. The word spread quietly from man to man, and none of us said anything to Red, or let on that we knew. It happened he was the only Jew in our platoon, and if we were overrun that afternoon, who would want the letter "H" on his own dog tags?

By now, the lack of more than a few minutes sleep at a time for five consecutive nights was affecting us in strange ways. A man would be talking to you, and then stop right in the middle of what he was saying, and you'd see he was asleep.

Determined to save their pocket west of the Rhine, and with plenty of ammunition, the krauts were still throwing in heavy barrages of artillery and mortar fire. But finally, their infantry losses had become insupportable, and they hadn't gained more than six hundred yards in five days of heavy fighting.

On the sixth day, the krauts abandoned the village ahead. Our square with its empty shell casings, darkened blood and blasted cobblestones was silent. We were all much older. Zellenberg had been seared into our memories forever.

Their loss at Colmar had been a significant defeat for the Germans, who withdrew across the Rhine in that area. The fighting had also been very costly for our side. Audie Murphy, whose Division took the town of Colmar, states in his book that "In 7 weeks the 3rd Division... suffered over 4,500 casualties". We had taken 11 casualties in our platoon of 34 men in our five Colmar days.

Fred G. Rand, Jr:

Late one afternoon when we were attached to a Battalion of the 45th Division, I was up at the OP, just firing some registration shots as I did most afternoons. These were only one or two rounds each on areas such as a ravine or a path that might be used by an enemy patrol at night. I would number each of these targets on a map overlay for ourselves and also for the Infantry unit we were attached to. In case they detected some need, the Infantry could then ask for fire at #1, #2, etc.

This particular afternoon a Lieutenant Colonel and another 45th officer came up to the OP and introduced themselves. The Lieutenant Colonel explained that he had always wanted to experience fire direction with the 4.2s, and would I let them fire a round or two? I explained what I was doing, how these map locations were passed on for their use, etc. My radio operator and I then told the people at the guns that there would be someone else asking for fire, and cautioned that if their request seemed to be incorrect, do not fire but question it.

Then I handed the Lieutenant Colonel the phone. After he called for two or three of these registration rounds, the officers thanked us and left. Some days later, Lieutenant Woomer asked me to go with him to the 45th Headquarters, for some reason. While there, I picked up and read a copy of the 45th newsletter that came out of their Headquarters periodically. In this copy was a story saying that this same Lieutenant Colonel had just been awarded a Silver Star when the attached mortar forward observer and the radio operator had been killed. It reported how the Lieutenant Colonel with complete disregard for his own life, had picked up the radio, called for and directed mortar fire, and broke up an enemy attack. As I was showing this article to Woomer, the Lieutenant Colonel walked in and was being congratulated by those in the room. I started toward him and for some reason, he looked at me and left quite hurriedly.

My radio operator and I had never realized how rapidly he and I could recover after having been killed!

Also, I had never known that just firing registration rounds was worth a Silver Star. Since I hadn't kept a very good record of how many days I had fired such rounds, it would be hard to estimate how many of these Silver Stars I should ask for!

Winter Fighting

Andrew C. Leech:

We advanced pretty rapidly and took several towns after shelling them quite a bit. We were shifted from this sector, on over to the extreme left flank.

Before we had time to unload anything and set up, we were attacked from the mountains. They came running down off the mountain yelling and hollering and shooting. They opened up with machine guns and burp guns all around us.

We were ordered to evacuate the town as we had not unloaded our vehicles. We jumped on them and raced through the town with bullets flying everywhere. They had the road leading out of town under direct fire, as we had to run through a stream of tracer bullets as we left town. We lost one man and had one or two wounded, and one was captured.

We found there were about three battalions of SS troops that took the town. We began shelling the town, but stopped because the Jerries had captured about 100 men of ours and were holding them in a church. So we were not allowed to shell the town.

There were so many wounded lying around that the Jerry medics sent a man out with a white flag to ask for blood plasma, dressings, and first aid for their men, and agreed to treat ours too. We sent it to them, but sent a doctor and some medics along to help care for the men.

In the meantime our troops surrounded the town but they had bitter house-to-house fighting trying to take it. Our prisoners were freed, but the town was a wreck and both sides lost heavily with dead lying all around.

We moved on, and set up in about a three foot snow. It was "some cold" but the fighting was limited to patrolling. We even went deer hunting in the snow behind our lines in the forest and killed several deer.

Sam Kweskin:

HOW I ENJOYED MY LEAVE, AND WHY IT GAVE ME THE TROTS:
I finally received a pass to take some R&R in Nancy. I welcomed the opportunity to wander through the streets of a large city to see what I could pick up — by way of anything newsworthy, you must understand.

I kept muttering French phrases to myself, practicing what I thought might be beneficial. "Alo! Comment-allez vous? Est-ce que vous voudriez une biere? Volez-vous diner avec moi?" and so on.

We arrived late. We were led to an unfinished building, standing like a concrete shell, and were shown to the second floor where one of the rooms was an improvised dorm, and our mattress — the concrete floor! But, hey! We *did* have a blanket or two with us, didn't we? And we were not on the front, right? Golly, gee! We even had a movie shown to us that night!

Early the following day, I sauntered through the city of rococco palaces and wide boulevards but if I dared walk up a side street, there seemed to be MPs coming out of the wood-work, shoving me back onto the main thoroughfare with waving batons. Thus did they attempt to prevent anyone from meeting anyone else which might eventually necessitate a visit to the "green room", otherwise known as the prophylactic station.

What to do? I didn't cherish the thought of sitting in a bar until ten or eleven at night, so I walked hastily back to my sumptuous surroundings, found my musette bag, rifle, helmet, and a blanket, and grabbed a recent edition of "Stars and Stripes". Then I flagged down a two and a half ton truck heading north.

According to the map the Third Army was immediately north of us, in and beyond this province of Lorraine. My next decision was to find one of two high-school buddies, one serving as a Piper Cub observer, and the other in the Infantry, both with the 70th Division.

Eventually I had to jump from the truck and wave down another driver heading northeast. After a while, I felt I had ridden in or on every known vehicle in the ETO, less a camel, when I hitched a ride in a command car. Thanks to a fatherly oak-leaf Colonel, his driver brought us to a fork in the road, at which point the Colonel said "We turn left here, son. Hope you find your friends!"

Now there was no vehicular traffic, and I hitched up my gear and began to walk within a forest, looking for moss on tree barks to learn where north was. About half an hour's walk brought me to a village, its name long since forgotten.

Strangely, there was no one walking in its streets, nor was there anyone peeking from a window. There was no sound except that of my shoes. Now with my carbine in both hands, I looked around, and couldn't even make out a lamp behind a window.

Fear of the unknown kept me from knocking on a door, or calling out. I went on, out of the village, continuing northeast.

After another mile or so, I began to hear cannonading. Alongside the road I saw a sign which read "883rd F A" adorned with an arrow. Now, beyond a curve in that road, there was a vast meadow with about four or five howitzers firing. I walked up to one of the GIs and asked if he knew a Private Granat.

"Max? Sure. If he's not up in the air right now, he bunks in that farmhouse down there."

At the edge of the meadow sat a farmhouse, easily about a hundred years old. As I looked into one of the rooms, I recognized one of the two fellows I was looking for.

"Hey, Granat!" I shouted. He turned. "Jeez! What the hell YOU doing here?" All the facts of my being with the 7th Army further south, the intervals between letters, and bits of information about one another only having come from our folks, he said "I don't believe it. It IS you isn't it? You came up TO THE FRONT on a PASS?" he asked unbelieving. I told him, after all, he was my best friend, why wouldn't I?

Strangely, there was no one walking in its streets,
nor was there anyone peeking from a window.

His buddy that asked "How did you get here?" So I told them about the rides in trucks, straddling a gasoline tank behind the cab, jeeps, a tank, and — finally — the Colonel's command car.

"Then," I said, "I walked through this eerie village, about a mile or two down that (here I pointed) road."

Both my friend and his battery mate, leaning against the wall, now sank to the floor. Max sat silently shaking his head, emitting an occasional chuckle.

"What?" I asked, not comprehending their general silence. "What?"

"That village," Max began. "That village — we haven't taken it yet!"

The epilogue to this story is that I left the following day on a hitched ride via a different, circuitous road, back to Nancy, hosting for the week that followed, a case of psychic diarrhea.

Unknown to us at the time, was the fact that our other friend whom I sought, was already dead, a victim of a German infantry incursion which overran a hospital into which he had checked as a "walking wounded".

Lee Steedle:

On the 20th of December our Battalion reorganized at Hagenau, just about 20 miles north of Strasbourg. Our losses had been heavy. But instead of having to pull way back and retrain a big batch of new men, we utilized our remaining strength. Our "D" Company officers and·men were transferred to "A" and "B" Companies. The 83rd now had only three companies, instead for four.

By now, although there was still a "hierarchy of oldness", we were all veterans. We had men whose ways we knew. We could depend upon one another. The nightmare of having had to use that lot of defective ammunition was now behind us.

After showers, plenty of beer and schnapps, and a couple of good days of hot food and relaxation, we were rested and ready to go again.

Christmas Eve found us not far from the German border in a tiny town, possibly Niederbronn. Its most notable feature was the big old church, which had lost most of its windows and a large part of its roof to shelling. When dusk settled upon the town, so did an almost eerie silence. There was no whumping of mortar shells, no brrrrp of machine gun fire, no low rumbling of engines. Silence. From somewhere in the officer echelons high and distant from us, there must have come an order. On Jerry's side too, someone must have passed a warning not to fire unless fired upon.

The local priest seemed to have known something about this, the Germans having just pulled out the day before. He invited those of us GIs who cared to attend, to a Christmas Eve Mass in his now open-air church. That was a memorable Mass, with men in overcoats, rifles slung from shoulders, flickering candlelight, and foggy breaths visible in the chilly air from scarcely-remembered carols. The sound of a single shot could have changed everything, but it never came. A blessedly silent night, but not totally dark. Occasional wary star-shells from both sides starkly illuminated the streets and rooftops. Jerry stayed peacefully on his own side of the narrow, quiet stream separating us. It was a night to realize Jerry was mortal and human, just like us.

Christmas, a day without gunfire, was almost but not quite the same. There was the rumbling of trucks and whining of jeep engines, the sounds of resupply. Both sides breathing and waiting. We didn't have to wait long for the move. It came from Jerry.

Christmas Eve Mass...rifles slung from shoulders,
flickering candlelight...foggy breaths visible in chilly air.

Our "B" Company platoon was overrun on New Year's Eve at Bitche, on the German border. We had been deployed so thinly that immediately in front of our platoon there was only a strong-point in the forest road, held by a stretched-out 45th Division Infantry platoon, and by a couple of lightly-armored recon cars.

We had been firing straight ahead for about two hours close to midnight, when the Jerries broke through not to our front, but on our right flank. They had overcome a recon car position and were moving toward us on that same dirt road along which we had been resupplied. After heavy firing, our baseplates always dug themselves deeply into the ground, and removing or shifting them required considerable shoveling. We had no time to either shift our baseplates or evacuate the mortars.

With heavy small-arms fire coming in, we had to pull back. We always carried a thermite incendiary grenade in each squad, so that we could destroy our mortars to prevent their being used against us. In the confusion, Sam Romeo another squad leader, hadn't heard the order. I found his grenade and dropped it down his barrel, after destroying my own.

Beyond the edge of the clearing our BAR man turned back, set his bipod, and fired into our big ammunition pile stacked just off the road. Every fifth round in his clip was armor-piercing, and he directed his fire accurately at our white-phosphorus shells. One of these ruptured, sending a white fiery spray over our gun position, igniting the other WP shells, which quickly cooked the high explosive rounds, causing our entire abandoned position to erupt in thunderous explosions. The WP smoke effectively covered our withdrawal, and for a time prevented the Jerries from bringing vehicles down our road. They paused and spread their infantry through the trees.

Withdrawing, we had the advantage of the road, while the Jerries were shuffling through about eight inches of snow.

This gave our platoon time to reassemble and occupy a shallow defensive ditch at a dirt crossroad 1,000 yards downslope. It was impossible for us to hold there. We had just experienced the opening of a 10-division German assault that pushed our Seventh Army back almost daily. By January 10th our front had lost seven miles.

All of our moves during those ten days were defensive. We grew accustomed to seeing Army Engineers taping blocks of TNT to the trunks of trees lining our forest roads. I recall one morning when we were ordered to fire a heavy barrage of both HE and WP in a wide arc, not with specific targets, but just so the noise and smoke of our shelling would cover the sound of dozens of trees being blasted to form a roadblock.

Up north, the German drive that pushed forty miles into Belgium, and that became known as the Battle of the Bulge, was finally turned back, as was the incursion on our own Seventh Army front. They marked the last gasp of the Wehrmacht as a formidable fighting force. The Germans had thrown everything they had into these attacks, hoping, we later learned, for a favorable negotiated peace with the Western Allies, rather than with the Russians. When their drives failed, they had little left, and no manpower reserves. The only real power remaining to them was emotional — they were defending their Vaterland, and they sometimes fought desperately as their resources crumbled.

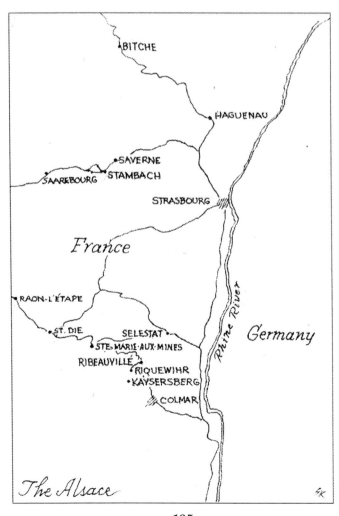

The Alsace

Last Fighting Days

Andrew C. Leech:

We started racing toward the Rhine River, taking hundreds of prisoners as we went.

I want to mention a colored TD battalion — the 614th TDs — that spearheaded the attack and did a swell job. They ran into several battalions of horsedrawn artillery and really shot them up — leaving men and horses scattered all along the road for miles. One German battalion surrendered to them intact, and the others that were lucky enough to get away ran off to the hills and left horses and artillery pieces behind. We helped round them up and bring them in to the prison camps that were then bulging. This roadside scene of destruction was really something to see.

From here we pushed on to the Rhine. We sneaked into a little town on the banks of the Rhine one night and laid down a barrage for a fake landing across the river. There were 22 batteries of American artillery concentrated in this area and the barrage lasted from 11:00 p.m. to 1:00 a.m. It was really terrific. I don't suppose there was much left across the Rhine where this was concentrated.

While this was just a fake to throw the enemy off, the 7th Army sent a task force across several miles below. We were then assigned to the 36th Division to hold the bank of the Rhine. We moved up to a town named Speyer on the Rhine and fired across the river for a few days. Then on April 2nd, we ourselves moved across the Rhine.

Frederick W. Endlein:

We were in Germany, going through a small town, in a convoy. Leading were some Infantry scout cars and some tanks. You could hear small arms fire, and some larger guns being fired. Then everything became disorganized, and we were told to get off the road and take cover. My squad and I took cover behind a farm house.

After things quieted down some, they moved us to another farm house where we set up our mortar behind the house.

What had happened earlier was that some Germans had an 88 in the bend of the road, and had knocked out our scout cars and some tanks. Now our Infantry was fighting house to house.

We were firing our mortar at the shortest range possible. We fired so much that we had to wrap rags around the barrel and pour water on it to keep it cool. One shell misfired and didn't come out of the barrel. After we extracted this shell, we found that the cone at the bottom of the barrel had become so flat, it wouldn't strike the firing pin on the shell. After changing the barrel we resumed firing. With our support, the Infantry repelled the counterattack.

William C. Ford

In the middle of March, "C" Company was attached to the 397th Regiment of the 100th Division as we advanced toward Heilbronn, Germany. It was still bitterly cold weather. As we moved through some towns the women civilians would observe our movement with frowns on their faces. Old men stood and stared at us. We could tell by their expressions that they could not accept Germany's defeat. Some elements of the German Army were still determined not to accept defeat, and were ready to fight to their deaths.

We moved toward Heilbronn on the Neckar River. Heilbronn was a stronghold, and still very important center to the enemy. We found outposts waiting for us in concrete pillboxes. We came under mortar and automatic weapons fire, and had a very bitter fight.

The 397th Infantry's mission was to cross the Neckar there at Heilbronn. As they began their attack, we laid thousands of rounds of HE and WP shells into Heilbronn.

The enemy had blown the bridge. As our Army Engineers tried to rebuild it, accurate enemy artillery fire would knock the bridge out before it could be completed.

We had orders to destroy every Heilbronn building edging the river. Many of these were people's homes. We would shell each house until it fell, then move our barrels to level another house, until all were destroyed.

Soon the Engineers were able to complete the bridge, and our forces crossed it into the city. Some amphibious tanks crossed at other points. The rifle company ahead of us fought hard to hold on, and was fighting from house to house, which was mostly rubble. Snipers were hidden everywhere in the torn down houses, but soon reinforcements arrived and cleaned out the town.

We advanced to Heidelberg, where many of the German officers had been trained in its University. None of the university buildings were damaged, as our Infantry cleared the enemy from each building. I entered one and saw a book written in English.

I had not read or even seen an English-language book in two and a half years. I picked it up, began to thumb through it, and came across a paragraph with all lines underscored.

It read something like this: During the Revolutionary War in America, General Washington was riding his horse along the front lines. Washington noticed a sergeant and his men trying to move an artillery gun across a high cliff. General Washington asked the sergeant what the trouble was. The sergeant replied: "Sir, I am having trouble getting this gun across the cliff, where I can continue to fire on the enemy". The sergeant added "If I only had one more man, I could move this gun." Then General Washington got down off his horse, put his shoulder against the artillery piece along with the others, and they were able to move the gun into a position where it could continue firing. The article then went on to say that regardless of how high you are in rank, always be willing to lend a helping hand when needed. I will always remember this statement. I think it is a very good practice for any leader to follow.

We would shell each house until it fell.

Lee Steedle:

The Jerries were moving back so fast that we sometimes lost contact with them, as they gave up huge stretches of flat land they no longer had the strength to defend.

One afternoon we were halted by a blown railroad bridge. The Engineers laid down a pontoon bridge beside it, but armored units and infantry had crossing priority, and we were told to occupy a nearby house, since we wouldn't be moving across until morning.

Dozens of railroad boxcars had been trapped on our side of the river. Having time and curiosity, several of our men broke into a few of them. In one, they were lucky to find our greatest treasure of the war — an entire boxcar filled with wooden cases of fine cognac and champagne. Liquid wealth beyond our wildest dreams! The Jerries had looted them from the French, and now here we were with all that great stuff, and we had to do justice to it in only one afternoon and night. We all tried valiantly, each man holding and guzzling his own bottle as though it were Coke.

Midway through that evening, someone remembered a grudge we had against the other platoon. All four of our squads went roaring down the stairs to the first floor, and our night ended with a glorious fistfight. The next morning, I had to tie one of the men in my squad onto a jeep trailer, to get him across the bridge.

Our 83rd P.O.W.'s Freed

Robert F. Thorpe:
From Torino, the Germans moved us to Stalag 7A, and made us work in the Munich railroad yards. We worked 30 straight days, and rode boxcars to and from the prison camp — a distance of about 25 miles. Our first food each day was a bowl of soup. The railroad people fed us lunch, and our supper back at camp was a bowl of cabbage soup.

We went through many bombings, day and night. One day, as a small air raid shelter started caving in on us, we got out and ran to another one.

In November, I was beaten by a guard with the stock of his rifle. I lost 45 pounds in prison camp.

In January, 1945 we were sent to a town below Nurnberg to build a narrow-gauge railroad. We left there April 21st, and were marched for nine days. We watched bridges being blown up by Germans south of Regensburg. Finally, on May 1st, we were liberated.

Lloyd L. Fiscus:
In January, 1945, we had been transferred to Rohrbach to build a 16-mile narrow-gauge railroad. New barracks were built, and about 100 men began the labor. Most of the Company "C" men captured at Briançon were in the group. The camp sat on a hillside overlooking the valley below, where we had completed probably a mile of tracks. As good American GIs we goofed as much as we could, and were accused of "sabotage" almost every day.

As the American front got closer, we began to see more of our airplanes. One day a group of our fighter planes came over and began strafing a German convoy passing on the road below us. It must have been Sunday, because we were all locked in our compound. I think that is the first time I saw our new P-5l Mustangs.

One day, one of the planes flew over us very low and waved his wings to us, after we had covered the roofs with white toilet paper spelling out "P O W". We later learned that the planes from this group were piloted by Afro-Americans.

At night, we were locked in our barracks, with a large pail to use for body waste. In the morning we would dump it in the outside latrine. To make this possible, a slit-trench was dug leading to the latrine pit. Well, one time when our planes were strafing, my friend Norman

141

Switching yard...favorite target of the U.S. Army Air Corps.

Brann dived into the slit trench. Since he was six feet tall, and the nasty fluid in the trench was only five feet deep, at least his head was above the nasty liquid. When things quieted down, I saw what had happened, and Norm was yelling for help. Well, we got him out of that mess, and convinced a guard to open the gate, and we took him down to a creek below the camp to clean up.

Dale C. Blank:

The transport that took us from Milan to Stalag 7A consisted of railroad box cars into which they put from 60 to 70 men, with little room to sit much less lie down. Going to the bathroom consisted of urinating in a boot, and pouring it out the small opening in the top of the wall at either end of the boxcar. We were not well fed so we didn't defecate very much, but the process was the same. Stops were erratic, and not to any schedule that we could discern.

The P.O.W. group consisted of soldiers from other American units, and some British soldiers. Stalag 7A had prisoners from all nationalities — French, British, Russian, Polish, Romanians and a whole bunch more. During our stay at 7A, we Privates were assigned work details on farms and other jobs.

Some of us were unlucky enough to be sent to Munich to work on the huge switching yard which was a favorite target of the U.S. Army Air Corps. We ex-P.O.W.s know what it means to be a slave.

Once in a while we would get a Red Cross Parcel to split with other prisoners. During my stay with the Germans, my body weight dropped from 165 to about 125 pounds; and my legs and body from the waist down had infected flea bites, some of which were as large as a quarter. We didn't get enough food to fight the infections, and the Germans did not have any medicine that would help.

After several months at Stalag 7A, 200 American prisoners were shipped to a small work camp near Rohrbach, to build a narrow-gauge railway to connect two major railroads so that German military supplies could be shipped more efficiently. My job was drilling holes in boulders so the Germans could blast them out of the way. I tried to explain to them that I had trained in demolition and could handle the whole job, but they declined and did the blasting themselves. I got the feeling that they didn't trust me. Imagine that.

Once on a detail to a German farm, Norman Brann — the same man who had jumped into the latrine during an air raid — was using a wheelbarrow to pile potatoes. A fat German Colonel pulled out his pistol and held it to Norm's chest. The Colonel was screaming all the time, and he tried to get the pistol's safety off so he could shoot Brann. It seems that Brann was running over the potatoes with the wheelbarrow and damaging them. This Colonel was livid with rage and couldn't operate the firearm. That's the only thing that saved Brann's life. Another German officer intervened and saved the situation.

We were ordered to be prepared to depart the camp and march to the east toward the Russians. We could hear the big guns from the front and knew the Americans were not too far away. Well they did take us out of camp and marched us to the east. At night we would sleep in barns or haystacks or anywhere we could, to keep warm.

Once we met another column of men who wore political prisoners' clothes. The two columns stopped, and the guards in the other group started beating on the prisoners, and then they shot a number of them, for no reason that we could tell. The prisoners were not causing any trouble that was apparent.

Finally, after two or three weeks, our guards told us that they had to leave us to be found by the American Army at a farm. We talked about half of our guards into staying with us for their own safety. These were old men about 75 to 85 years old, and they didn't need to be cannon-fodder for the Germans. I'm sure these guards were better off than those who left us to continue the fight.

The morning after the guards told us they had to leave, we were *free*. A lone GI with a beautiful blue neckerchief came up the hill and was our liberating force. I wish I would have gotten his name and outfit. We were so excited that we forgot everything. I think he was from the 80th Division. No matter, to us he looked like the Angel Gabriel.

Three of us left almost immediately and started to go west, because that was the way home. We had breakfast at what looked like a community kitchen, which was operated by three women. While we were eating, an ex-political prisoner came to the door and asked for food, so I made the German women feed him and give him some extra food to take along. This man got down on his knees and kissed my hand, which embarrassed and humbled me.

We three *EX-PRISONERS* (I still like the sound of that) then liberated three bicycles from the local population and started west.

The Liberation of Dachau

William C. Ford:

On April 29th we were advancing toward Munich after taking a number of smaller towns. On that day, the 157th Infantry Regiment of the 45th Division, with our "C" Company in support, reached the Dachau Prison Camp. Staff/Sergeant Robert S. White and his squad of the 157th were the first troops to open the prison gate and disarm the SS guards. I did not go inside the prison myself, but only watched just outside the gate.

Staff/Sergeant White's rifle squad took the SS guards' weapons and stacked them by the gate. A camp prisoner walked over, picked up one of the stacked weapons, and fired on the SS, wounding one of them. Just one, before he was disarmed.

We moved closer to the prison gate and saw how very poor and sick some of the prisoners were. Some looked like only skin stretched over their bones. Some were too weak to walk out the gate to freedom. It was a terrible sight to see.

SS guards disarmed at Dachau's gate.

Andrew C. Leech:

The most pathetic thing of all: we liberated a large concentration camp near Munich (Dachau), and it was unbelievable to see the condition these people were in. They were walking skeletons. They had no food, and very little clothing, which was tattering about them.

They said they hadn't had anything to eat in about eight days. We sat down in groups, as we were in position firing on the next town. And when we got time we took down our own rations, built fires, and cooked them for these people. They ate it and told some awful weird stories in the meantime. When they had finished, they thanked us and wobbled off toward the road which was about a hundred yards away. Two of them fell dead by the time they reached the road.

Sam Kweskin:

I got to the edge of the railroad line, across the road from the walled entrance to the Dachau camp. The "40&8" boxcar touching the concrete pylon at the end of the rail tracks held grey and blue prison uniforms.

At the corner of the parallel street on which we stopped our jeep were two "street signs". One of these, meticulously carved, painted, and varnished, showed two SS guards holding a Semitic-looking character, his feet off the ground. The other sign said "To the SS Barracks".

I asked an elderly woman whose house was just across the road from the camp, its doorway facing the boxcars, if — since 1933 — she had seen any people removed from the train and marched into the gate. To all my questions, she answered "I know nothing!"

Dale C. Blank:

We three *EX-PRISONERS* rode our liberated bikes awhile, and then at Regensburg liberated a very small van-type truck which was too small to put our bikes in, so they were left behind.

We drove to Dachau, and couldn't believe what we were seeing. Picture train flatcars with human bodies piled on top of each other like cordwood. These people all looked like they had starved to death. There was nothing to them but skin and bones, no flesh, no fat, no nothing.

In the camp, the rest of the people were in little better condition. They looked at us with those sunken eyes that I can see to this day. At that moment I knew what we were fighting for. Naziism was the worst thing that could have happened to this world.

Shortly before we arrived at Dachau, American MPs brought two SS troopers to the camp. The prisoners somehow gained possession of the two SS, and beat them nearly to death. The MPs put the SS troopers out of their misery with bullets to the head. The smell of the place was death itself.

These prisoners had been used to work in the factories around the town of Dachau, yet the German people in the town said they knew nothing about the concentration camp, although it was right there for all to see. If you wanted to know what Hell was like, camps like these all over Germany and the occupied countries were the places to visit. The American Army should have destroyed every city and all the people in them that had one of these camps.

While driving around the town of Dachau, we saw a civilian car going down the road, and we followed it to its destination, which was a private home. After he stopped, the German proceeded to remove a washing machine from the car. This guy had been out scavenging.

We three GIs talked it over and decided that a car would be more comfortable and suit our free status better than the truck, so we persuaded the German to trade us vehicles. He was somewhat reluctant to trade, but in a short time he came around to our way of thinking.

As it turned out, the car had a bad starter, and had to be pushed to start the engine. It was no problem for me, because I was the full-time driver, but my friends objected after awhile because every time we stopped the engine they had to push again.

One of the guys suggested we go back and get our truck, so we did just that. But this time I took the car, and my friends took the truck. Now the German really got hostile, but it did him no good, after all we were the victors in this war and we knew that we deserved the spoils. So after explaining to him that we may do him some harm, he saw it our way and went into his house without further outbursts. None of us were in any mood to take any crap from any of the Germans in the town of Dachau, after we saw what they did to those prisoners. Anyhow we thought that maybe this was a start of his rehabilitation to re-enter the human race.

Rolling To The End

Andrew C. Leech:

We next headed south toward the Brenner Pass and Austria. Again we rode day and night. Every house had a bed sheet or white flag of some description hanging out the window, and the civilians and children were all standing outside waving white handkerchiefs.

Former German soldiers kept coming out of cellars and marched out to the road with their hands up to give up. No one had time to bother with them, so we just motioned them back to the rear of the column. It was a steady stream of them day and night marching to the rear of our column with their hands over their heads and no one guarding them at all.

It was really a sight to see the little children. In many cases, after seeing the German soldiers coming out with hands over their heads, they thought they were supposed to do the same. Imagine cute little kids with their hands over their heads shouting "Kamerad!"

Wofford L. Jackson:

I almost got in serious trouble near Garmisch. We had just raided a Nazi house and loaded a 6x6 truck with a thousand bottles of champagne and cherry brandy. The Germans were big on cherry brandy. A British Major came up to me and said "Sergeant, where is your requisition for this champagne?" I pulled out the trench knife that I had got from Renfroe. I said "Here's my requisition!" About that time, a Pfc. replacement drew his gun on the Major and said "Let me kill him, Sergeant, let me kill him!" The Major took off one way, and we went the other. When I think of this now it scares me to death.

Fred G. Rand:

Until a German General surrendered Innsbruck, Austria, my platoon was part of a task force attached to a battalion of the 103rd Infantry Division. Of course, we were moving along small roads in the Alps — not the autobahn. At some place along the route we were stopped while the Engineers repaired a bad spot in the road ahead. Since we were so high up in the Alps a cold wind was blowing and it was snowing.

We had rigged a shelter half to protect us in our jeep from the wind, while someone was cooking Ten-in-One rations inside.

While we were sitting beside the road with our seven vehicles with 83G painted on the bumpers, I heard someone hollering:
"Who is in charge of these 'G' vehicles?" "Up front, sir!" Then again, "Who is in charge of these 'G' vehicles?" Again, "Up front, sir!"

By this time I had unhooked the wind-shielding shelter half, and stood beside the jeep. One of my men was sitting in the back seat, frying bacon in a skillet over a Coleman stove.

General McAuliff, who had said "NUTS!" to the Germans at Bastogne, was now the Commanding Officer of the 103rd Infantry Division. He came up beside me and asked if I was in charge of these "G" vehicles? I saluted, stood at attention and replied "Yes sir!"

"What the hell does this 'G' stand for?" the General inquired. I said "Well sir, the 'G' actually stands for gas, but we are..." "Gas? What the hell do we have gas vehicles for, way up here?"

Here I am, a Lieutenant standing at attention in front of a General, when the man sitting in the jeep frying bacon, spoke up and said: "Why General, when you have vehicles, you have to have gas!" Then General McAuliffe answered "That's right, son — well, carry on!", and he left.

"What the hell does this 'G' stand for?" the General inquired.

Later on, General McAuliffe became head of the Chemical Corps. Probably when this conversation took place, he did not know that 4.2 mortars were in the Chemical Warfare Service, and that we naturally had "83G" on all our vehicle bumpers. That is the story of just one of many times when someone important, whose troops must often have counted on 4.2 mortar fire support, didn't know that our 4.2s were in the CWS!

Innsbruck...they had surrendered to us.

It's Over At Last!

Andrew C. Leech:

We reached the outskirts of Innsbruck, Austria. We were met there by a German General who told us he would lead us through the town, and that they had surrendered to us.

We climbed aboard our tanks and vehicles and rode on into town.

The streets of Innsbruck were lined with people waving Austrian flags and waving at us. We took over the town and confiscated a hotel or two, and made ready to get some much needed rest.

It was here that we got the order to cease firing and to remain where we were. The Germans in the 7th Army sector had surrendered! Then, within a short time came the surrender of the remaining German forces to the Allies.

I guess you people back in the States celebrated what you called VE-Day. Well, it was just another day with us, and it took quite some time for us to realize there was no more fighting for us to do.

Frederick W. Endlein:

When the war ended we were in Austria in a little village called Kolsass. We stayed there and did some policing up of some stray Germans that were hiding in the mountains.

Up in the hills were some dairies where they would make swiss cheese; for a pack of cigarettes they would give you a huge slice of cheese and a glass of milk.

Douglas A. Swayze:

The Battalion had a raffle: A 10-day trip to Berne, Basel, Lausanne, St. Moritz, and Geneva — all as guests of the Swiss Government. Hastings (Company "C") and I won.

Wonderful! Except that the first night in a barracks in Strasbourg my wallet with $300 was stolen. I had no identification, or orders, or money. I borrowed $10; bought a carton of cigarettes, sold it for $20; sold my field jacket for $40; and now had $60. Enough. The Swiss treated us to everything — we were the first GIs to visit that country.

On the way back I missed my train and had to hitch-hike all the way back to Austria. No identification, no orders; but no one, no MP, questioned or stopped me. I was always afraid I'd be picked up as

Captain Edwards reads awards presented by General Waite, Chief of CWS.

AWOL. I was two days late getting back. Again, no one doubted me. Quite an experience!

Robert B. Smith:

(Excerpt from June 27, 1945 letter to his wife Annette):
I lose the entire Company tomorrow morning. The old "Longbow Charlie" will be no more. Of course... it's not the original bunch that started overseas together. There have been 145 killed in action in the Company since it started, and of course, many more than that wounded to varying degrees, so we couldn't expect the original bunch to all be with us. I told the boys "goodbye" last night at Retreat formation. The outfit I slept in the same holes with, and sweated out the same shellfire with, are gone now. I guess I'm kinda tired.

Wofford L. Jackson:

I was discharged at Camp Gordon, where we started. The people in charge started talking about re-enlisting, or the Reserves. I said "Stop, stop! Don't say another word. When I get my civilian suit and my knife and fork back, and turn in this damn spoon, you won't be seeing me ever again. My wife is waiting for me at the Richmond Hotel!"

William C. Ford:

There are some things we must never let ourselves forget. Remember each of us who carried on the fight without wavering.

Let us never forget the two years of continuous combat. North Africa, and our aggressive training and team work under Colonel Darby's Rangers. The amphibious assault on the beach at Gela, Sicily. The amphibious assault on the beach at Cape Orlando. The amphibious assault at Salerno, Italy. The high peaks at Chiunzi Pass, and on into Naples. The Volturno River crossing. The hard fighting at Venafro and the Cassino line. The amphibious assault on the beach at Anzio; and the sinking of our LST 544. The hard fight to capture Rome.

Then came the amphibious assault on the beach at Ste. Maxime, Southern France; and the "D" Company glider landing at Le Muy. Remember the three rivers in the Vosges Valley. The Colmar fighting, and the action in Alsace. The crossing of the River Rhine. The bitter fighting at the Siegfried Line. Then the drive toward Munich, where we helped capture the infamous Dachau concentration camp. Finally, our advance into Austria, where the war ended.

Remember all the men who paid so heavily. Let us not forget our buddies, our friends who gave their lives for the blessings we enjoy in our Country. Remember the trail of blood which those white Crosses and Stars on foreign soil represent: Americans who gave their lives to maintain the American heritage.

I will always remember the great pride we all had for our unit: The 83rd Chemical Mortar Battalion. *NEVER FORGET!*

Awards

Rounds Away,
the official history of the
83rd Chemical Mortar Battalion
reports that during
508 days of combat
these awards were earned
for distinguished service:

3 Distinguished Service Crosses (Posthumous)

2 Legions of Merit

39 Silver Stars

9 Soldiers Medals

97 Bronze Stars

5 Croix de Guerre

876 Purple Hearts

91 Oak Leaf Clusters

Mark Freedom **PAID**

HEADQUARTERS SEVENTH ARMY
WESTERN MILITARY DISTRICT
APO 758   US Army

GENERAL ORDERS)   16 November 1945

NUMBER   647)

COMPANY "C", 83D CHEMICAL MORTAR BATTALION, for outstanding
performance of duty in action against the enemy from 10 to 27
September 1943, near Chuinzi Pass, Italy. This company landed at
Maori, Italy, with the Ranger Force on the night of September 8 and
9, 1943 with the mission of seizing the high ground controlling
Chuinzi Pass and to secure the left flank of the Fifth Army.
The holding of this position was vital for flank security, for
observation on the plains of Naples, and observation on German supply
routes and communications lines to the Solerno battlefront.
During this period, Company "C" exhibited unusual gallantry and
determination in man-handling mortars and supplies to mountain tops.
the men worked continuously, night and day, keeping the unit
supplied. Mortar crews were cut down to one and two men per gun, and
the remaining men fought with the Rangers and went on combat patrols.
Subjected to almost continuous mortar and artillery fire and
repeatedly attacked by a determined, numerically superior enemy,
Company "C" maintained extremely heavy fire and filled in all gaps in
the ranger line. Company "C" men fought side by side with the rangers
using their automatic weapons and grenades with devastating effect.
Company "C" mortar fire was of necessity brought to within 50 yards
of friendly units as seven major counterattacks were repelled during
the period, and numerous enemy patrols were stopped, often in bitter,
close-in fighting. Company "C"'s mortars kept the German Army supply
route under continuous effective fire although the supply route was
two thousand yards beyond the authorized range. The men and officers
of Company "C" displayed extraordinary determination in supplying
their mortars, which were at the top of the mountain, with ammunition
and spare mortar parts. Despite limited food and water supplies, and
the continuous nature of enemy fire and activity, this company
maintained its courage and determination throughout an extended
onslaught by an enemy determined to wipe out its positions and made
possible the successful accomplishment of a vital mission.

BY COMMAND OF LIEUTENANT GENERAL KEYES:

JOHN M. WILLEMS
Brigadier General, GSC

OFFICIAL:

W.G. Caldwell
Colonel, AGD
Adjutant General

Mark Freedom **PAID**

R E S T R I C T E D

HEADQUARTERS SEVENTH ARMY
WESTERN MILITARY DISTRICT
APO 758   US Army

GENERAL ORDERS   )   16 November 1945

NUMBER   648   )

COMPANY "B", 83D CHEMICAL MORTAR BATTALION, for outstanding
performance of duty in action against the enemy from 15 to 21
February 1944, near Anzio, Italy. When the enemy attacked with a
numerically superior number of troops, tanks and artillery, Company
"B" advanced down Anzio Road through intense hostile barrages and
contacted the leading American unit. The company knowingly occupied a
position which had been previously held by two other organizations
that had been driven from this area by enemy action. Exhibiting great
determination in maintaining this position as superior German forces
infiltrated between Company "B" and the infantry, the unit received
enemy artillery fire which produced direct hits on two mortars and
destroyed ammunition. Small arms and mortar fire was heavy and the
enemy continued to press forward on the right. Contact could not be
regained with the infantry, and the enemy began advancing on all
sides. Under cover of the security elements, the company worked its
way south to an overpass to an alternate position and, with much
effort, saved all usable mortars. Enemy infiltration increased as did
enemy fire. Mortars were again set up. As the enemy attack continued,
constant mortar fire was placed upon the hostile infantry and tanks,
producing many casualties. Unceasing enemy artillery and rocket
barrages knocked out guns and crews. Enemy dive bombers bombed the
position again and again, communications were continuously disrupted
and yet mortar fire was maintained continuously against the advancing
enemy and tanks. As the Germans succeeded in driving between the
157th Infantry and the 159th Infantry Regiments, Company "B" prepared
to meet the attack on the overpass, working with the British Loyals.
The enemy advanced through "B" Company's withering mortar fire north
of the overpass and was engaged on the overpass by the Loyals in
hand-to-hand fighting. The company then aided the British and engaged
infiltrating enemy forces on the flanks and the rear.
During this action the Loyals and Company "B" were the only combat
units between the enemy and Anzio. Several hours later, a battalion
of Gordons, obtained from quartermaster and service units, was placed
in a defensive line to the rear of Company "B". As this enemy
attack was broken, others were begun and Company "B" continued its
concentration on the enemy. Despite the lack of food and water
supplies, and the continuous nature of enemy fire and air activity,
this unit maintained its courage and determination throughout
the difficult periods and assured the completion of a vitally
important mission.

BY COMMAND OF LIEUTENANT GENERAL KEYES:

JOHN M. WILLEMS
Brigadier General, GSC

OFFICIAL:

W.G. Caldwell
Colonel, AGD
Adjutant General

Mark Freedom **PAID**

GO 122

General Orders

WAR DEPARTMENT
Washington D.C., 22 December 1945

BATTLE HONORS. -- As Authorized by Executive Order 9396 (sec. I, WD Bul. 22, 1943), in the name of the President of the United States as public evidence of deserved honor and distinction. The citation reads as follows: General Orders 657, Headquarters Seventh Army, 20 November, 1945, as approved by the Commanding General, United States Army Forces, European Theatre.

Company D, 83rd Chemical Mortar battalion is cited for outstanding performance of duty in action against the enemy from 9 to 27 September 1943, near Vietri-sul-Mare, Italy. This company landed on a heavily mined beach with a Commando force on the night of 8 to 9 September 1943, with the mission of seizing high ground controlling Vietri-pass and to secure the left flank of the Fifth Army. The holding of this position was vital for flank security and for observation on the German supply routes and communication lines to the Solerno battlefront. The company executed the difficult landing in the face of small-arms and tank fire. Mortar crews were cut down to one and two men per gun, and the remaining men fought with the Rangers and went on combat patrols. When aggressive enemy attacks advanced to within the minimum range of the mortars, the men of Company D went forward into the lines with the Commandos and used their grenades, small arms, and automatic weapons with devastating effect. During this period, Company D was subjected to almost continuous mortar and artillery fire, and repeatedly attacked by a determined enemy. By great ingenuity, enemy armored attacks were repelled and the supply route for the Commando and Ranger Force was kept open. Raiding parties against the enemy were very successful; and when Commando casualties could not be handled by the understrength Commandos, men of Company D volunteered and evacuated the wounded under fire. During the height of the action, Company D was firing into the west, the north, the east and southeast. Only the sea to the rear was clear of the enemy. the main line of resistance was never more than 1,000 yards from the beach. Upon receiving relief from the British Commandos, Company D took part in the action at Chiunzi Pass with the ranger Force. Again Company D cut its mortar crews down to two or three men and went forward to fight beside the Rangers. Mortar fire was, of necessity, brought to within 50 yards of front line units as serious attacks were repelled. Both men and officers displayed extraordinary determination and doggedness in supplying their mortars, which were at the top of the mountains, with ammunition and spare mortar parts. Although they fought without rest or relief and with limited food and water, the courageous members of company D offset enemy superiority and made possible the successful accomplishment of a vital mission.

Mark Freedom **PAID**

About our Contributors

Dale C. Blank:
Private, "C" Company, in Lieutenant James Doyle's platoon, Tony Defeo's squad. Awarded Purple Heart and Prisoner of War medals. Army service: April '43 to December '45. Wife: Patricia; four children. Retired real estate broker. Hobby: photography.

George R. Borkhuis:
Staff/Sergeant. Mess Sergeant, "D" Company; later Hq. Company. Awarded Purple Heart. Army service: March '42 to September '45. Member original cadre, 83rd. 47 years with Chase Manhattan Bank. Subsequently worked for foreign exchange house 2 years, then an animal boarding kennel 9 years. Moved to Duluth, MN, July '96. Hobby: stamp collecting.

Samuel M. Bundy, Jr.:
Deceased. Corporal, "A" Company Clerk. Army service: August, '42 to October, '45. Joined 83rd October, '42. Contributions in this Anthology condensed from his wartime diary. Worked for Wanamaker's department store, Philadelphia; and later for Jimmy Swaggert.

John M. Butler:
Tech-5, "A" Company motor pool. Army service: April, '42 through September, '45. Joined 83rd, 1942. Worked 28 years for Esterbrook Pen Co.; then Owens Corning, 14 years. Retired '84. Married three times; four step-children. Hobby: Travel, has gone three times around world. Comment: "Can't understand why 83rd didn't deserve combat recognition".

Michael P. Codega:
First Sergeant, "D" and later Hq. Companies. Awarded Bronze Star, Soldier's Medal, and Purple Heart with Oak Leaf Cluster. Army service: April, '42 through October, '45. Member, original cadre of 83rd. B.S. Providence College. Married to Helen 47 years. five children: three sons, two daughters. Owned motel, Old Forge, N.Y.; later municipal auditor, Pittsfield, Mass. Retired, March '81.

Andrew J. Connolly:

First Lieutenant, received battlefield commission. "A" and "C" Companies. Awarded Bronze Star with Oak Leaf Cluster. Army service from July, '42 through April, '45. Joined 83rd July, '42. Joined Cml. Res. Corps. Worked for N.Y. Daily News. Recalled into Korean War with 477th Cml. Service Bn., served until April, '53. Married. Son. Retired '81. Comment: "Very proud to have been part of 83rd — there is a closeness that we hold today for one another that words cannot express."

Robert E. Edwards:

Captain, Headquarters Company. Army service from March, '42 through April, '62. Promoted to Major. Awarded Purple Heart with Oak Leaf Cluster. Civilian life: ran Edwards True Value Hardware for 27 years, retired '73. two children, five grandchildren. Plays duplicate bridge. Memories: The hasty retreat down Mt. Vesuvius; Venafro; the loss of the Rangers; the loss of 216 83rd members in the LST sinking; the most popular operation in the Army: circumcision!

Sam Efnor, Jr.:

Lieutenant Colonel. Entered Army '40, served through June, "61, retired as Colonel. Joined 83rd as Commanding Officer at Anzio. Married Ann Pennington, December, '41. Two sons, David William, and Samuel Jeffrey. Retired, living in Salt Lake City. Comment: "I commend all contributors for this book effort".

Frederick W. Endlein:

Sergeant, "B" Company, Squad Leader. Army service from July, '42 through September, '45. Joined 83rd in first filler group. Married 50 years; have a son and daughter; two grandsons. Worked 31 years as electrician; retired 1984.

Lloyd L. Fiscus:

Private First Class, "C" Company, Sergeant Norm Wahaski's squad. Awarded Prisoner of War Medal. Army service from April '43 through December, '45. Joined 83rd February, '44. Recalled to active duty for Korean War, '50. Was married 51 years, wife Dolores died January, 1997. Has 2 sons, 9 grandchildren, 3 great-grandchildren. Retired after 40 years as Vice President, Boviard Company.
Comment: "Enjoy biennial reunions of 83rd."

William C. Ford:

Sergeant, "C" Company, First Platoon. Squad Leader. Awarded Bronze Star with Oak Leaf Cluster; Purple Heart. Entered service September '42, joined 83rd October, '42, discharged as Staff Sergeant, September, '45. Plans to celebrate 50th Wedding Anniversary with wife Mary, in November, '97. Son: William, Jr.; three grandchildren. Worked 33 years, U.S. Postal Service, retired 1990.

William Gallagher:

Sergeant, "A" Company, First Platoon, Communications Squad. Awarded Purple Heart. Army service from September, '42 through April, '46. Joined 83rd October, '42. Married; have son, daughter, four grandchildren. Returned to work for DuPont postwar, continued with company for 45 years. Retired in '86.

Morton Gorowsky:

Private, "B" Company. Sergeant Kimbrough's squad. Army service from April '43 through November '45. Joined 83rd December '43. Wife, Shirley; have two boys. Worked in milk industry 35 years. Retired 10 years.

James G. Helsel:

Corporal, "A" Company, Second Platoon, Third Squad. Awarded Purple Heart. Entered service October, '42, joined 83rd same month, discharged September, '45. Comment: "Thankful I joined 83rd — sincerely believe I couldn't have met a nicer group of men."

Raymond "Pop" Hoover:

Corporal, "B" Company, later Headquarters Company Awarded Silver Star, Bronze Star, Purple Heart. Served four years in Cavalry pre-war; re-enlisted in 1941 at the age of 32. Was one of three brothers serving in Italy. Married Kathryn. Son, William, two grandchildren.

Wofford "Woof-Woof" Jackson:

Staff/Sergeant, Platoon Sergeant "D" then later "A" Company. Entered service September '42, joined 83rd October, '42, discharged October '45. Awarded Bronze Star and Purple Heart. Married, two daughters, two grandsons. Served 20 years in Manchester, Georgia city and county governments. Active in many civic and veterans organizations; and a lifetime Church Deacon.

Sam Kweskin:

Private, "D" and Headquarters Companies. Awarded Croix de Guerre serving with 3rd Chml. Mortar Bn. Army service from February '43 to December '45. Joined 83rd September '44; was 83rd's combat artist for *Muzzleblasts* and *Rounds Away*. Divorced. Three children (one deceased); four grandchildren. Art Institute of Chicago, BFA; Illustrator; Advertising Agency Art Director; TV cartoonist; Medical Illustrator; Marvel Comics artist '49—'92. Presently doing portrait commissions. Comment: "Glad to contribute illustrations and maps for this book!"

Andrew C. Leech:

Deceased, May, 1990. Private First Class. "B" Company BAR-man. Army service from October '42 through November '45. Contributions in this book condensed from wartime diary and his later book: *WWII Experiences of Andrew Candler Leech*. Married Earline Kuykendall; two children, Alice and Douglas. Alice presently serving as Vice-President, 83rd Veterans Assn. Andrew was Teacher, Coach, and County Welfare Director. Retired in August, 1973.

John P. McEvoy:

Major, Headquarters Company. Entered Army service April '42, joined 83rd July '42; rejoined Army in '47 following a civilian sabbatical. Completed service in July, '66, as full Colonel. He and wife Edie have three daughters and four granddaughters. Comment: "The education in character and courage given by the experiences and the friends of the 83rd have guided my life. We are the lucky ones."

Julian "Mac" McKinnon:

First Lieutenant, "C" Company, 2nd Platoon. Awarded Bronze Star, Soldier's Medal, Purple Heart. Army service from July '42 through March, '46. Joined 83rd September, '42. Later promoted to Captain. Married Florence, have three children. Worked 38 years for Proctor and Gamble Co., in manufacturing management. Retired 1984. Hobbies: sailing, traveling, maintaining house built in 1820. Comment: "Our reunions are the highlight of the year."

Lawrence H. Powell:

Corporal, "A" Company. Entered service September '42, joined 83rd that October, discharged October '45. Married 50 years, have two daughters. Worked 39 years as pipefitter, retired 1985. Hobbies: arts and crafts, golfing, bowling. Comment: "Enjoying seeing fellows from our outfit at the reunions."

Fred G. Rand, Jr.:

First Lieutenant, "A", "D" and "B" Companies. Awarded Purple Heart. Army service from January '43 through May '46. Joined 83rd July '44. Grade at separation: Captain. Remained in Army Reserve; retired as Colonel after 32 ½ years active and reserve duty. Married LaVerne in '48; two daughters, two grandchildren. Worked as Chemical Engineer, Olin and Mobil Fertilizer Plant, 35 years. Retired in 1981.

Perry B. Rice:

First Lieutenant, "D" then "B" Company. Platoon Leader. Entered service, March '42, joined 83rd July '43, completed service December '45. Awarded Bronze Star, Purple Heart. Married to Ann McGinness 47 years, have four daughters. Worked for Arnold Bakers, Inc., as Assistant Controller/Credit Manager. Retired April 1985. Sport: tennis.

Robert B. Smith:

Deceased, 1959. Captain, "C" Company Commander. Entered service August '42, joined 83rd at Anzio, April '44, left service May '47 as Major. Awarded Silver Star, Bronze Star. Contributions in this book were condensed from wartime letters to wife Annette. Postwar owner and operator of a motor supply company; was President and Director of Hot Springs National Bank.

Robert L. Sorensen:

Tech-4, Medical Detachment. Awarded Purple Heart. Enlisted February '42, served through September '45. Joined 83rd at its activation. Tech-3 at separation. 4 children, 3 grandchildren. M.A. Psychiatric Social Work; 40 years Director Mental Health clinic.

Lee "Young-un" Steedle:

Sergeant, "D" then "B" Company. Squad Leader. Awarded Purple Heart. Enlisted November '42, joined 83rd March '44, discharged November '45. Married to Alice Pandolfi 46 years; have five sons, two daughters, nine grandchildren. Advertising agency copywriter; international marketing director Reader's Digest, worked in 35 countries. Retired '81. Hobbies: writing; making gargoyles and creative art fountains. Comment: "Enjoyed editing this Anthology."

Douglas A. Swayze:

Tech-4, Medical Detachment. Awarded Purple Heart. Army service
from October '42, when joined 83rd, discharged September '45.
Following WWII married Marie Halman; have two step-children.
Had a men's shop for 28 years. Retired for 20 years.

Robert F. Thorpe:

Private. Headquarters Company, then "C" Company radio-man, F.O.
Awarded Prisoner of War Medal. Worked 11 years Mechanicsburg
Naval Supply Depot, Penna.; did airconditioning service for 37 years.

Reno L. Toniolo:

Staff/Sergeant, "A" Company, Platoon Sergeant. Awarded Bronze Star.
Joined Army October '42, and 83rd same month. Discharged October
'45. Married Evelyn Wolfe, October '45; have two children, nine
grandchildren, seven great-grandchildren. Partner in auto parts
business — went from one store with 6 employees to 21 stores with
250 employees. Presently President, 83rd Veterans Association.
Hobbies: Singing and guitar playing; making custom wooden
furniture and jewelry boxes.

Edward L. Trey:

Captain; served with Headquarters Company and later "B" Company,
as Forward Observer. Awarded Bronze Star and Purple Heart.
Entered service February '41, joined 83rd May '42.
Married, with five children.